C000194837

NAJAF MAZARI was born in 1971 in a small village near Mazar-e-Sharif in northern Afghanistan. At the age of 12, he left school and, unbeknown to his parents, apprenticed himself to a master rugmaker. Thus began his love affair with rugs.

He fled Afghanistan in 2001 after being tortured, narrowly escaping certain death during the genocide of Hazara men and boys in Mazar-e-Sharif carried out by the Taliban. Reluctantly leaving behind a young wife and six-month-old baby, he made the dangerous journey overland, eventually crossing the ocean in a leaky boat to the shores of Australia, where he ended up in the Woomera Detention Centre. After his release, he settled in Melbourne where he now owns a rug shop, selling traditional Afghan rugs.

His wife and daughter were finally given permission by the Australian government to join him in 2006 after almost six years' separation. In April 2007, he was granted Australian citizenship.

ROBERT HILLMAN is a Melbourne-based writer of fiction and biography. His most recent biography, *My Life as a Traitor*, written with Zarha Ghahramani, came out in 2007 and appeared in numerous overseas editions the following year. His 2004 autobiography, *The Boy in the Green Suit*, won the Australian National Biography Award for 2005.

His collaboration with Najaf Mazari on *The Rugmaker of Mazar-e-Sharif* grew out of an abiding interest in the hardships and triumphs of refugees.

THE RUGMAKER OF MAZAR-E-SHARÍF

Najaf Mazari & Robert Hillman

*But the real and lasting victories
are those of peace, and not of war.*

Emerson

insight

Published by Insight Publications
219 Glenhuntly Road
Elsternwick Victoria 3185
Australia.

Tel: +61 3 9523 0044
Fax: +61 3 9523 2044
Email: books@insightpublications.com.au
www.insightpublications.com.au

ABN 57 005 102 983

First published by Insight Publications in 2008, reprinted 2008, 2009
Text copyright © Insight Publications 2008

Cover and text design: Susannah Low
Authors' photo: Tim Mullane
Front cover photo of Najaf Mazari: Lara McKinley
Maps: Dimitrios Propokis
Editing: Catharine Retter, Robert Beardwood & Iris Breuer
Printed in Australia by Ligare Book Printer

National Library of Australia
Cataloguing-in-Publication data:

Mazari, Najaf, 1971-
The rugmaker of Mazar-e-Sharif / a memoir
of Najaf Mazari written by Robert Hillman.
Elsternwick, Vic.: Insight Publications, 2008.
9781921088551 (pbk.)

Mazari, Najaf.
Woomera Immigration Reception and Processing Centre.
Refugees--Australia--Biography.
Afghans--Australia--Biography.

Hillman, Robert, 1948-

325.2109581

DEDICATION

*This book is dedicated to all those people
of Afghanistan who have lost so much
in wars – their houses, their limbs and
their lives – and to all people working for
peace throughout the world.*

NAJAF'S JOURNEY

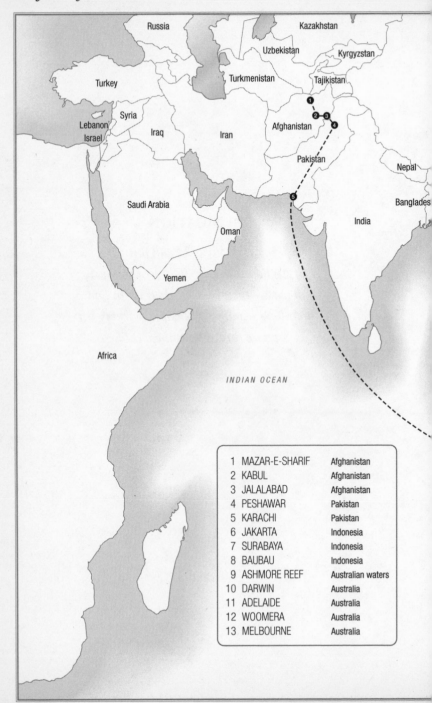

Russia

Kazakhstan

Uzbekistan

Kyrgyzstan

Turkey

Turkmenistan

Tajikistan

Lebanon
Syria

Israel

Iraq

Iran

Afghanistan

Pakistan

Nepal

Saudi Arabia

Bangladesh

Oman

India

Yemen

Africa

INDIAN OCEAN

1	MAZAR-E-SHARIF	Afghanistan
2	KABUL	Afghanistan
3	JALALABAD	Afghanistan
4	PESHAWAR	Pakistan
5	KARACHI	Pakistan
6	JAKARTA	Indonesia
7	SURABAYA	Indonesia
8	BAUBAU	Indonesia
9	ASHMORE REEF	Australian waters
10	DARWIN	Australia
11	ADELAIDE	Australia
12	WOOMERA	Australia
13	MELBOURNE	Australia

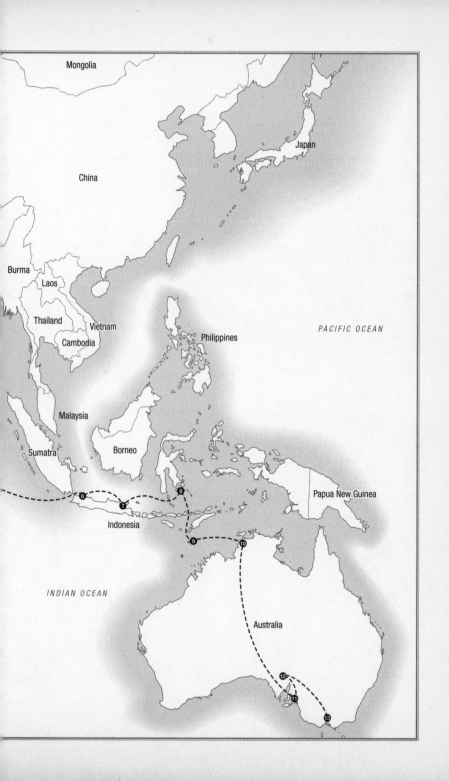

CONTENTS

1

Singing in the Wilderness

I DID NOT KNOW that I could feel this much sorrow without a body to bury. How heartsick can I become before I break down and weep in front of everyone? I wander about the camp with the blanket from my bed around my shoulders, searching for a spot where I can't be seen and can't be heard. And where would that be? I have been in the camp for three months. If such a spot exists, wouldn't I have discovered it before this day?

The camp is Woomera, or really my small part of Woomera, a section called November. I share November with hundreds of people from lands I have never visited, lands that are as mysterious to me as my own homeland of Afghanistan is to the guards who keep watch on us day and night.

We who are watched and guarded, we who are questioned, probed, doubted—we are all illegals. We have come to Australia without invitation. We have jumped the queue. I had not heard an expression like that before I came to Australia—'jumping the queue'. It belongs to communities that place a very high value on orderliness, on due process. It's a good thing, of course, to value orderliness. The community of Afghanistan is only orderly now and again. But it was never my intention to jump this strange queue of which I had never heard. I don't think any of us here ever thought of stealing our way to the head of a long line of people patiently waiting to cross a border into Australia. Most of us would never have qualified for a place in the long line to start with. All I wanted to do was to stand up on the soil of a land where rockets did not land on my house in the middle of the night and hold my arms wide and say, 'Here I am. My name is Najaf Mazari. Do you have a use for me in this country?'

As I wander between buildings, I catch sight of the desert beyond the wire fences. I come from a land of deserts, but this desert is not the same as those of Afghanistan. It is difficult to say in what way it is different, but it is. If I were to fall asleep in the desert of Afghanistan without a soul in sight and somehow wake in the desert of Woomera, I would know in an instant that I was in a strange place. It is not only my eyes that would tell me, but my skin. The touch of the air itself would whisper it to me. My skin has lived all but six months of its 30 years inside a few square kilometres of Afghanistan.

I find a solitary place at last. I am in an alley, concrete beneath my feet. Before me stand tall steel bars dividing the compound—in which I am free to walk—from a building housing an office of the Department of Immigration. I have been in that office, but only once. I sat in a chair at a metal desk. An official of the Immigration Department took a seat behind the desk. An interpreter sat to my right. The official spread papers and documents on the surface of the table. Some of the documents were mine, but they did not include a birth certificate. I have never had a birth certificate. Back in Mazar-e-Sharif, I have a taskera, which is more like a family history going back for ages. But no birth certificate. Very few Afghanis can produce such a document. What a country I come from! Strangers to the idea of queue-jumping, and on top of that, babies are born without anything in writing to prove that they exist!

I sit with my back against the wall of a building on my side of the bars and close my ears and eyes to all sounds and sights except for those inside my head. This is July, bitterly cold here in Australia, hot in northern Afghanistan. I see a sky full of stars—northern hemisphere stars. I see a moon above the dark outline of mountain peaks. I see a woman—my mother—setting plates on a cloth. I see the face of my older brother, Abdul Ali, and I see his stern gaze fixed on another face. The other face is mine, a much younger face than the one I wear now. I see a field of grass as high as a man's knees, dotted with wildflowers of red and yellow. Now the sky I see is blue and the face I am staring at is that of my sister, Latifeh. She's smiling, not just at me but at everything. I hear voices calling from a distance across a field. I hear the barking of our family dog, also a long way off. In this mood that combines despair and rapture, I begin to sing.

The song that finds its way to my lips is one that is sung at New Year by the Hazari of Afghanistan. New Year in the Afghan calendar falls in March when there is a hint of the coming spring in the air. Hamal is the first month in our new year, a word that can also mean 'pregnant'. Flowers are beginning to bloom at that time, bright red flowers with delicate petals. The song is usually sung by shepherds. I am not a shepherd but a rugmaker;

I have never sung it before in my life, although I have listened to it many times. I lift my head and send the words of the song into the air of Woomera. Perhaps this is the first time that these words and this tune have been heard in this land, unless some earlier Afghani attempted it. Afghanis came to Australia many years ago; they came here to work—more than 100 years ago, so I have heard.

So I sing. The words tell a story of youthful love and desire, and the mood is that of longing. I don't think of anything as I sing, but the words feel sweet on my lips, like the juice of some over-ripe fruit. It is a pleasure to use my native tongue in this way, exploring the shadows of language. There is very little poetry to enjoy during a normal day in camp.

> *Come and let us go to Mazar, dear Mullah Mohammad,*
> *To see the field of tulips. Oh, my sweetheart!*
>
> *Go, tell my beloved, "Your lover has come;*
> *Oh beautiful narcissus, your suitor has come."*
>
> *Go, tell my beloved, "Good news, your beloved has returned;*
> *Your faithful lover has arrived."*
>
> *Come and let us go to Mazar, dear Mullah Mohammad,*
> *To see the field of tulips. Oh, my sweetheart!*
>
> *Come, oh my sweetheart, I am mad with love for you.*
> *I am destroyed, longing for your ruby red lips.*
>
> *I don't kiss the rim of the wine goblet;*
> *I am in anguish and I am heartsick for you.*
>
> *Come and let us go to Mazar, dear Mullah Mohammad,*
> *To see the field of tulips. Oh, my sweetheart!*

Before I have finished the song, I become aware of a group of immigration officers watching and listening from the balcony of the building beyond the steel bars. They must have heard my song from their office, then stepped out onto the balcony to search out the source. A glance tells me that they are listening with pleasure. There are smiles on their faces. Naturally, I stop singing when I notice them. It is not because of embarrassment that I stop, although that is partly true; it is because the song is a private matter between me and the heartsickness that drove me to seek out solitude.

The interpreter who was in the office with me for my interview some months back is amongst the officers listening from the balcony. He calls down to me, 'Sing it again! It's beautiful!'

But I shake my head. 'I can't,' I say, in Dari.

The officers ask him to ask me again, but again I shake my head and this time make a brief explanation in Dari.

'I am not a singer.'

Once this is interpreted, some of the officers nod, understanding my reluctance to continue; others make a gesture with their hands and shoulders as if to say, 'Such a pity.'

The officers and the interpreter drift back into their office. I gather my blanket around my shoulders and shuffle back to the dormitory. On the way, it strikes me that all the words I had employed in my long interview with the immigration officer and everything I have said to the officers and guards since, have not made a fraction of the impact on them as my song. For a few minutes, I was not merely one of hundreds of down-at-heel nuisances from some hellhole in Central Asia, but a man with something to offer, a song to sing and maybe a tale to tell that might be worth listening to; a tale that might even be true.

I have not lost the burden of my sorrow by the time I reach the dormitory, but its weight is a little more endurable. Maybe these Australians will let me become a complete man again. Maybe they will let me use my brains and muscles and heart and soul in some worthwhile way. What do I know of life? I know that life is work. I know that a man rolls up his sleeves and labours. I know that he must preserve his dreams.

For the first time in months, I can hope. And it's good to feel hope come to life again in my heart. I think of the red flowers around the mosque at Mazar-e-Sharif. I think of how they bloom each year, no matter how many rockets explode over them.

2

Fire in the Night

I AM ABOUT TO tell the story of an explosion, or really, the story of two explosions and of the deaths that followed.

Like almost every Afghani, I have witnessed a number of explosions in my lifetime, always unwillingly. Afghanistan has been a type of explosion laboratory over the past three decades. In the 1980s, the Russians tried out bombs and exploding devices in Afghanistan that came fresh off the drawing board. We Afghanis had the undesired honour of being among the first human beings on earth to be blown to pieces by this state-of-the-art Russian weaponry. The mujahedin, the sworn enemies of the Russians, also had very up-to-date mortars, bombs, mines and rockets, provided by the Americans and the Saudis. The arsenal of the Taliban came from all over the world; whatever they could buy, they used. When the Americans bombed the Taliban (and many people who had nothing to do with the Taliban) after the destruction of New York's Twin Towers, Afghanis once again enjoyed the awful privilege of being killed by ultra-modern high explosives. I have had the opportunity all my life—not that I ever desired it—to gaze at the impact of explosions on buildings, machinery, bridges, streets, the countryside itself and on human beings. Whatever the damage to buildings caused by explosives—and it is an ugly thing to look at, homes that once had the honest task of keeping the rain off people's heads now standing like decayed anthills in the desert—the buildings can be created again, and the bridges and the mosques. The old tinsmith I saw in the marketplace of Mazar-e-Sharif turned inside out by a mortar explosion could not be remade. When people are broken as badly as that man, or as badly as many others I have seen—old men, young men, mothers, small children—they are beyond fixing, all of them.

My family moved to the city of Mazar-e-Sharif in 1980. We had been living in the small village of Shar Shar high in the mountains up until the time of my father's death, and would have continued to live there as long as my father desired. The decision to move to Mazar-e-Sharif was made by my older brother Gorg Ali, who became the head of the family once my father had died. It was his plan to build two houses on a large block of land just inside the gates of the city and settle there for the rest of his days. What he had in mind was a small farm where he would keep a few cattle and harvest the orchard that already existed on the site. It was to be a type of paradise, on a small scale. The land itself was family property through my father's marriage to the second of his two wives.

Let me tell you a little about Mazar-e-Sharif itself. It's a small city by world standards, but fairly big for Afghanistan. It had a population of 110,000, while the largest city in Afghanistan, the capital, Kabul, had shrunk from 1.3 million people to no more than 700,000 people by 1988, with all the troubles in our country. Afghanis are a people of the outdoors, by and large. We farm, we herd livestock, we grow crops, we mine gems, we keep orchards. Almost 80 per cent of all Afghanis make their living by growing, harvesting, digging and herding. Even the traditional Afghan trade so close to my heart, rug-making, is sometimes carried out in the open air. So we Afghanis have never been an urban people, never relished living in bustling cities. In many ways, we are the people we were hundreds of years ago, and even hundreds of years before that.

Mazar-e-Sharif is in the far north of the country, close to the borders of Uzbekistan and Tajikistan. To reach the city from the south, you must either cross the mountains of the Hindu Kush that run deep through the heart of Afghanistan, or else go east from the Hazarajat (the age-old home of my people, the Hazara) then head north. That way, you skirt the heel of the mountains. Mazar-e-Sharif lies in the broad valley that falls away to the east in Turkmenistan and eventually subsides into the desert of Peski Karakumy. It's as cold as the arctic in winter, very hot in summer. The city is famous as the burial place of Ali, son-in-law of the Prophet, and is also the great centre of the Afghan rug trade—a fact that was to make the world of difference to the direction my life took.

We built two houses of mud brick on our 500 square metre block of land. The houses were erected along the western boundary, an Afghan version of what in Australia would be called semi-detached houses; a common wall, but separate dwellings. On the northern boundary stood a smaller house, a bungalow, for guests; a kitchen and tandoor; a woodshed and a stable. In the centre of the expanse between the two groups of buildings a pool was situated, overhung by a single tree. A pool such as ours was a feature of all Afghan homes, so long as the owners could afford it. And if you could manage a tree to spread its branches over the water of the pool, so much the better. For all Middle Eastern peoples, a pool of water is not just an ornament; it is a thing of beauty in itself and a symbol of the life that water makes possible. A separate small reservoir provided water for household use. This little reservoir was filled each week from a channel that flowed directly from the river. The entire block of land was surrounded on all sides by a high, mud-brick wall.

My family took pride in the home and life we had made for ourselves in Mazar-e-Sharif. Although we had not distanced ourselves from the fighting altogether, we were well away from the fiercest sites of battle in the south. We were not a family of political firebrands; we were suspicious of all the grand claims of salvation made by the government, by the Russians, by the mujahedin. For us, salvation meant a place where we could worship and work. We were a roll-your-sleeves-up family. We believed that people made themselves happy by working, saving, building, providing for the future. The Hazara had spent centuries fighting for their place on God's earth but it was never the sort of fighting that is fuelled by political ambition, the desire to build an empire, subjugate other people. My older brother, Gorg Ali, used to warn us to steer clear of all political parties, all political disputes. He had an instinctive distrust of fiery speeches, as if he could see that the passion and anger in the arguments of one political party simply aroused the same

10

sort of passion and anger in another party.

'Anger is a hammer,' he told me. 'It has only one task—to strike hard, and strike again. And your enemy's anger is just the same.'

I don't mean to say that he was without any convictions; no, it was just that he could see how easily people argued themselves into a situation that could only end with guns being loaded and knives being drawn.

At the time of the explosions that brought an end to this little paradise in the north, my family was made up of my older brother, Abdul Ali; a younger brother, Rosal Ali; my brother-in-law, Hassan, and my sister, Latifeh; Abdul Ali's wife, Zani-lala (as she was called); my mother; and myself—at 16 years old—the second youngest child. On the day of the explosions, we were feeling especially secure.

The President of Afghanistan, Babrak Karmal, had made a special visit to Mazar-e-Sharif probably at the insistence of the Russians, who controlled him. What the exact purpose of the visit was, we didn't know. Perhaps the Russians wanted to show that Karmal could roam the nation freely (he couldn't), or that he was very popular in the north (he wasn't). It would have all been to do with some strategy of the Russians, and really, of no interest to my family aside from the fact that Karmal was accompanied by a huge force of Russian troops, making it very unlikely that our region would see any fighting between the mujahedin and the Russian-backed government forces for a time, so we thought. In Afghanistan at that time, feeling secure was never a long-term thing; a few days of security, maybe a month, gave us the feeling of being on holiday. We enjoyed our meals a little more than usual; we joked more often; such simple things, but important. We'd heard some fighting during the day, but it was far off to the north. How much happier I would be now if I had taken some time to reflect on the nature of this civil war that had raged for five years up and down Afghanistan. For truly, it was impossible to feel safe when battles could change course in a matter of hours. Neither the Russian-backed government forces nor the mujahedin cared much about innocent bystanders. In fact, the whole category of 'innocent bystander' didn't exist in Afghanistan in the years of civil war. Both sides expected that it would be necessary to kill civilians, or at least that it would be too troublesome to avoid killing them. Neither side acted with any real conscience.

On the day of the explosions, it had been my intention to stay the night at my Uncle Ibrahim's house, some distance from my own home. Strangely, I found myself distracted and restless all that day, unable to settle. Instead of remaining with my uncle and his family, I made some excuse and began walking back home. The restlessness was all to do with a foreboding that hovered above me like the dark clouds of a winter sky. It was the type of foreboding that you want to be rid of, want to argue away; you tell yourself that it is all nonsense. I had known such forebodings before, sometimes in matters that were of no great importance, sometimes in matters of life and death. The forebodings are not mystical; I don't want to give the impression that I am gifted in some way. Indeed, I believe that many people experience these feelings, although not everyone pays as much attention to them as I do. I didn't believe that the troubled feeling in my heart was to do with the war, though. I had no idea what it was to do with. An animal foraging in the mountains will sometimes lift its head from grazing and look around to the north, the south, the east, the west. It has caught no scent, it has glimpsed nothing, yet some instinct has suddenly disturbed its peace. It returns to its grazing, a little unsettled. Some distance away, a hidden hunter fixes the crosshairs of his rifle sight on the head of the beast. The hunter's finger rests against the trigger. When he is ready, he will fire.

On my way home, I stopped at the Shrine of Ali to pay homage to the son-in-law of the Prophet. I kissed the shrine and prayed, hoping for some relief from the dark feelings that so plagued me. But there was no relief. It was now sundown. I said to myself, 'Ah, Najaf, what is it to be? Return home? Or should I go back to my uncle's house?' In the end, I turned my face toward home, tears of melancholy running down my face.

My mother was surprised to see me; she had expected me to remain at my uncle's house. And she could see that all was not well with me. She could see the sadness in my eyes, and the fearfulness.

'Is there trouble?' she asked me.

I didn't attempt to explain but instead glanced away, as if my thoughts were occupied in some other way. What could I have said that wouldn't distress her? Her heart was still broken after the death of Gorg Ali a year before, and would stay broken for the rest of her life. I had no desire to burden her even more.

We ate our evening meal together, gathered around the cloth on the floor that served as our dining area. Our meal was the common fare of evening in Afghanistan: rice, pallou, a beef curry, fresh bread, then very hot tea followed by the fruit of the season. Everything was normal in our household. We chatted, mentioned plans for the coming day, spoke of the visit of Karmal to the city, spoke a little of our belief that the mujahedin would keep to the mountains, wished each other a sound sleep and a safe awakening, and prepared for bed.

It was that period of summer when the nights remained hot. On such nights, it is the custom of Afghanis to sleep outdoors. My mother laid out toishaks—the cotton-filled mattresses that we use in Afghanistan—and erected a tent of mosquito netting above each. When I stretched out under my thin, summer blanket, I could hear the distant and muffled sounds of cannon fire in the mountains blending with the angry buzz of the thwarted mosquitoes hungering for my blood. Then in the heat of the night, I slept.

The noise of the first explosion was astonishingly loud. I had heard explosions before, of course—some nearby, some more distant—and I knew the sound they made. But this was far louder, I was inside this explosion. I heard the voice of my brother Abdul Ali raining curses on the head of Karmal, who had brought this catastrophe down on us. But that I was indeed in the midst of a catastrophe was something I had yet to fully understand. I attempted to get to my feet but found it impossible to make my legs obey my brain. My mother was screaming at the top of her voice, calling the names of her children.

'What has happened?' she cried. 'In the name of God, what has happened?'

I couldn't move. I gazed in horror at the devastation around me. My eardrums were aching. I saw Abdul Ali, Hassan and Zani-lala running in the direction from which my mother's cries were coming, running into the darkness. With that image fixed in my mind, I heard the long, shrieking sound of a rocket descending—a sound I knew. Even as I lay in my crippled state counting off the seconds before the rocket landed—I knew that five or six seconds would pass before impact—I could not make myself believe that this new disaster was intended for us; God would not permit it!

The second rocket exploded with an even more violent roar than the first. My ears ached as if scalded. I saw my mother running in the direction of the road, screaming for help from the neighbours. I saw the fingers of one of her hands hanging loose in a stream of blood. I saw one of my brother's cattle dead and torn in the rubble. I saw on the ground a human shape with a ragged, red hole where the chest should be. Of my brother Abdul Ali, I saw nothing. My hearing was gone.

Over the next few minutes, the images that reached my eyes were like those in a silent movie. Shapes appeared out of the silent darkness, then disappeared, reappeared, disappeared. Strange things were happening in my head. Images that had nothing to do with what was happening floated into my mind, then lapsed and drifted away: the sheep I used to tend as a boy; my father's body being prepared for burial; Gorg Ali peeling an apple with his knife, using only one hand.

It seemed to me that death was approaching like a visitor who would take up residence in my body and dull my pain and take away all my memories. As I waited for the visitor to arrive, a thought came to me with great force and clarity. For all I knew this was to be the final thought of my life.

Only poetry would do justice to that thought, but I offer it here to the reader with my apologies for lacking the skill to make it as vivid as it was at the time:

If I were the owner of a hundred palaces, they would
remain where they stand for I leave this world with just
the skin that is wrapped about my bones.

I am telling this story in 2006. The rockets exploded in 1985. In the 21 years that have passed since that night, I have returned countless times in my mind to the silent darkness and watched the shadowy figures growing closer to me, receding, swallowed by the night. I watch myself as if I were a spectator. I see myself lying at an angle across the toishek, the mosquito netting hanging in shreds. I can hear my very thoughts. 'Get to your feet, stand up, run for your life . . .' I see myself reaching down to wrench my legs into action. I see my hand held before my face, dark with blood. And then this strange film I am watching ends and my normal memory takes over.

I awoke in hospital. It took me a minute or more to understand this. My right leg was heavily bandaged. I was aware of pain, but what impressed itself on me even more than the pain was the contrast between this brightly lit room and the darkness of the night that I had escaped from.

Within a few minutes of regaining consciousness, my Uncle Ibrahim came quietly into the room and sat beside me in a chair. I could see from the expression on his face that he had something bad to tell me.

'Your brother Rosal Ali has been killed, God receive him,' he said. 'Hassan, too, has been killed, God receive his soul. Abdul Ali is badly wounded, but he will live. Your mother has suffered a terrible wound, but she too will survive, thank God. Latifeh and your sister-in-law have been spared, thank God for their safety. Alas, your home is destroyed.'

It took me hours of thought after Uncle Ibrahim had gone before I could properly understand what he had said to me. I could recall his exact words, but their meaning didn't come. When I understood at last, I cried out and moved my head from side to side on the pillow to make the meaning go away. But the meaning stayed. Again and again, I cried out. A doctor came and looked closely at my face, then shook his head and said, 'Be brave.'

I thought most of all of Rosal Ali. He had caused me so much anger when he lived, but that anger somehow made me love him more now than if he'd pleased me every day of his life. I had wanted to see him live long enough to become more responsible, to become a brother I could be proud of. I would not have the chance now to be proud of him. It hurt me deeply to know this.

In the days that followed, I lay in bed attempting to master the pain in my leg and the pain in my heart. That my mother and my older brother had survived was a blessing, and yet I could barely manage to think of my mother's agony at the death of my younger brother, coming only a year after the death of her firstborn son, Gorg Ali. I thought of many times in the past when both brothers were still alive. I wondered what my fate was to be in this land of Afghanistan, where war succeeded war. I had time, too, to recall my father's death many years earlier, and his funeral. That seemed the beginning of this journey I was on; this journey that asked so much of me and of my family.

3

Shoes

THERE IS AN AUSTRALIAN term I have heard and had explained to me, and it describes me as I am today, as I was yesterday and—without some big improvements—as I will be tomorrow. That term is 'sad sack'—somebody who's finding it difficult to smile; someone who looks as if the weight of the world rests on his shoulders. A sad sack is also somebody you might laugh at; not cruelly, but as if to say, 'Come on, it can't be as bad as all that.'

Well, it's true; it can't be as bad as all that. But here I am in Woomera with a big fence around me, a wife and a baby 5000 kilometres away, and only one shoe to my name. That's right, one shoe. Where is the other shoe? God alone knows. I lost it somewhere on the ocean. I walk about the November sector of Woomera with a long face, rain clouds over my head, and one shoe to share between my two feet. A sad sack.

I'm not normally a sad sack. In my family, I'm known as the cheerful one, the one who's always smiling. But it's difficult to be cheerful when I feel so powerless. To place your fate in the hands of other people is never a happy situation. People I do not know and who do not know me, except for a few little facts, have to decide if I am a fit person to take my place in the community of Australia. I wish I could show these people letters from people who knew me in Afghanistan; letters that would prove that I know how to earn a living.

'This is Najaf,' the letters might say. 'He has a fine wife and a beautiful little daughter. He pays his taxes. He doesn't shoot people. He mended a rug for me and did the best job you could imagine. He used to be a shepherd in the hills near Shar Shar. If the sheep could write, they would tell you that he took good care of them. Let him stay in your country. You won't regret it.'

Wandering about in my one shoe, I try to make myself useful. I asked for work, and the supervisor has found me a job in the kitchen. I get up early in the morning and make my way to the place where we go to eat our meals which they call the mess. There, I prepare the bread for breakfast, boil the eggs, put out the tea bags. It's not skilled work. The bread is in plastic packets, 32 white slices in each, and as I place ten slices on each plate at the centre of the tables, I think once more of the strangeness of this bread; it's like a distant cousin of the bread we eat in Afghanistan. I boil the eggs in big aluminium pots, one dozen eggs to a pot, cooked for exactly six minutes, by the clock. The tea bags are very new to me, too; each with its little string and tag. I always feel puzzled as I prepare breakfast, and also a little forlorn; this is not the way we eat in Afghanistan;

all the enjoyment is drained out of the experience. Foods such as these are not designed to be sold in bazaars but in supermarkets (I have heard of them).

Eighty people just like me searching for a new home in the world file past me with their trays, taking a mug for their tea and a boiled egg and some white sliced bread and a little piece of butter wrapped in tin foil (such a strange way to serve butter). I greet many of them in my own language of Dari, and those who speak a different language I smile at by way of greeting. When all of these hopeful refugees are seated at the mess-hall tables, I sip my own tea and watch them eating. Most were poor in their homelands, I would guess; most had put together the few thousand dollars needed to pay the people smugglers by borrowing or by taking a small store of bank notes from under a board in the floor. Some will be repaying the money they borrowed for years to come, and if they die, their relatives will have to pay.

Looking at these faces leaning forward as they rest their elbows on the tables and sip their tea, I think to myself that not one of these people would have gambled money in their lives. Not one would have borrowed in order to bet or to buy lottery tickets. But now they have all gambled every scrap of money they could put their hands on. I think of the odds for such a gamble. First, there is the journey by land, and that journey by itself can end in disaster, in capture or death. Then comes the journey by sea—even more dangerous. Then, November. Some of us will be permitted to stay, some will be sent away. It's a very bad gamble, a foolish gamble if you think about it. But if you are one of the winners, it's worth it. You can build a house that will not be blown up. You can work, and keep what you earn.

Life becomes possible.

Once breakfast is over, I help to clean up, wash dishes, wipe the tables, sweep the floor. When the work is over, I wander out into the compound to begin the day. I don't count serving breakfast as the beginning of the day, or not of the difficult part of the day. Serving breakfast is enjoyable; I can use my hands, I can be helpful, time passes quickly. But after breakfast comes the empty part. I stand under the same sky I stood under yesterday and look out on the same dry land. The tall fences that keep me inside this very small piece of Australia are the same fences that kept me inside yesterday, and the day before and for weeks stretching back. Has anything changed? Has my application moved from one desk to another somewhere in the city of Canberra? Has anything been written on my application by an important man—a tick, a cross, a question mark?

I imagine the important man in an expensive suit sitting at a big desk. Many applications rest before him. He has eaten his breakfast at his home in the city of Canberra. His children have dressed in their school uniforms and put lunches in their schoolbags. They have kissed him and said, 'Goodbye, father, do some good work today, and be happy.' They leave to catch the school bus, or perhaps they are close to the school and they can walk there on their two feet. The man in the suit has drunk his coffee and kissed his wife. She has made his tie straight, or maybe she wants him to change his tie for a better one, and she goes to find the better tie and makes him put it on. She is a good wife. She cares for how her husband will look when he goes to work. And now he sits at the big desk and takes a folder from the top of the pile. He opens the folder and looks at the picture of a man, or the picture of a woman. He reads the documents in the file. He picks up his pen and he writes something—a tick, a cross, a question mark...

Under the blue sky, I ask myself, 'Has anything changed? Has anything happened? Will this be a different day for me?'

On a square of barren ground, refugees are playing soccer. All the players on one team speak one language; on the other team, they speak a different language. They call to each other in Farsi, in Dari:

'Here, Haji, over here!'

'Quickly, this way! Quick!'

'Hey, use your brain, if God has given you a brain!'

As they play, their shoes raise puffs of dust. I watch on, smiling. If I had two shoes, I could join in. It will happen one day. I will become Two-shoe Najaf instead of One-shoe Najaf. But even more than a second shoe, I would love a cigarette. That would be happiness for a few minutes. A few months ago, before I was transferred to November, I cleaned the whole of the Town Hall in Darwin for the payment of two cigarettes. I knew I was being robbed, but it was very important to me to have those two cigarettes, one for now, one for later. Those who don't smoke have no idea how important it is to have a cigarette at certain times. They think, 'Why, that foolish man is doing harm to his body! He must stop.' But a cigarette can make you content for a few minutes when nothing else can. It gathers up all the pieces of your mind and body and knits them together. You think, 'Ah, well, they say the sun is about to fall from the sky and that will be the end of everything. So be it! I have five minutes before this disaster, and I will use it to smoke this last cigarette.'

Not having that cigarette I desire, I shuffle around the edge of the soccer pitch and stand in a different place and continue to watch the game. The sun overhead has moved a small distance on its journey across the sky. I look away from the game and wonder what I can think about to make the sun move faster. I have enough time in November to think about anything I want to think about. Such luxury! Possibly I will think about rugs, about the joy I feel when my eyes rest upon a fine rug, a true rug, made from the best wool, woven by a master. But no, it is not a good idea to think about rugs. If I do, I will make myself sad. I will want to touch the rug, feel the wool in my fingers, study the pattern, turn it over and study the craft of the weaver from the back. I will want to crouch down and gaze at the colours, and think of how the dyes were made, and from what substances the dyes were made, and whether the dyes do justice to the quality of the wool. I will want to brush the palm of my hand over the surface of the rug, and in doing so, my hand will tell me the whole story of the making of the rug, and the story will go straight into my heart. So I will not think of rugs. Not today.

Instead I will think of my wife and my baby girl. Or will I? That will make me sad all day. I want my wife to know that I have crossed thousands of kilometres of land and thousands of kilometres of sea and that I am still alive. I want to shout loud enough for Hakima to hear me in Afghanistan, 'I am here! I have found the land of Australia! It was over the ocean, just as it shows itself on the map!' And then I would shout a second time: 'A blessing on our daughter! Tell her I have seen no kangaroos!'

It's true; I have seen no kangaroos. I would like to see one. I would like to watch him leap.

So I have thought about what to think about and I think it is best to think of nothing just for now. It is safer. Sadness is like a stone in your shoe at a time when you can't stop to get the stone out. Each step you take, it bites your foot and soon tears come into your eyes.

Why am I talking about shoes so much? What sort of man spends so much time thinking of shoes? Be quiet about shoes, Najaf!

Still, a second shoe would be nice. I would like a second shoe.

❋ ❋ ❋

In the middle of the day, I go back to the kitchen and start preparing to serve lunch. The menu doesn't change much from day to day: rice with some chicken, or rice with some beef. I am glad I am being fed, yes, but it sometimes seems to me that the authorities who control the camp think that people who don't have white skin live entirely on rice. Rice is good, but there are other things just as good. Noodles are good. Noodles are cheap. I would like some noodles. And maybe some vegetables. Vegetables are good. But for the time being, there is just the rice and the chicken or the rice and the beef. Sometimes I get so bored that I feel interested to find out if it is chicken or beef we are serving today.

I serve out the rice and the chicken, making sure that everybody gets the same amount. There's always trouble when the amounts are not exactly the same. Because there are people here from five different countries, arguments grow into tiny wars. An Iranian gives a little more to his friends from Iran and immediately a Chechen complains. Then the Afghanis have to decide whether they are on the side of the Chechens or the Iranians. Probably they take the Chechens' side, since there are only two Chechens and they need some friends. Also, the Iranians have never really liked Afghanis. We Afghanis are the neighbours of the Iranians, but they make jokes about us and call us donkeys, only good for carrying things. So we think the Iranians are arrogant. November is the Middle East crowded into a very small space. If they keep us here long enough, there will probably be a war.

Serving food and cleaning up the kitchen is a task that Afghanis leave to women. If I had gone into the kitchen and started cooking food and serving it out in my home in Mazar-e-Sharif, my mother would have felt deeply insulted. She would probably have hit me with a saucepan. But here in November, serving food suits me very well. At least I am working. When you are raised to work hard all your life, you can never forget it. No matter how hard the work, you feel that God is watching you and saying, 'Yes, that's Najaf, he's a good worker, a good man.' Work repays your debt to God for making you a human being. You know, even if the Australian Government sends us all back to where we came from, it would be better if we could all work while we are waiting for a decision. Make us work, give us some pay. Build a factory at November. We could make things. Give us some machines and some leather and we could make shoes.

Aiee! Shoes again. Shoes, shoes, shoes. Enough!

Everybody has a plate of food now. When all of us refugees are eating at the tables, I like to imagine that the 80 of us all belong to the one family. It's not true, but for a few minutes each day, I like to think it is true. We are all Muslims; we have the one God, the one faith. Amongst the 80 of us there are wives and children, grandmothers and grandfathers, young men in their

25

twenties, older men in their thirties and forties, teenage boys, teenage girls, babies and small children. What is the difference between this man sitting at a table close to where I stand and my brother, Abdul Ali? They are of the same age. They are both of the Hazara. They even look alike. And the woman at the next table could just as well be my sister, Latifeh. Although we are not, all of us could easily be related to each other. We all have the same experiences, too. It was a mujahedin explosion that killed my younger brother but others here have had family members killed by Russian explosions in Chechnya, or Iraqi explosions in Kurdistan. We have all had to bury people we loved after battles that we did not start and did not want. And so I watch this big family eating and chattering and reaching for another square slice of the strange bread of Australia and some of them are beginning to eat the apples that are provided to finish the meal and it makes me happy for a few minutes. I like families. It is good for my heart to watch them eating, to enjoy my daydream.

After lunch, I begin to wander again. The strength in my body wants me to use it up, but I can't use it up. I can only shuffle about and look up at the sky to see if there are any different shapes in the clouds from those that were there ten minutes ago, and say 'Salaam' to Hassan, to Mohammad Ali, and 'Hello' to the guards and officials I come across. My English is getting a little better. I know the names of many things, now. Bread. Chicken. Beef. Apple. Table. Chair. Egg. Building. Man. Woman. How strange to think that there is a word for 'bread' in every language. Hundreds of words for 'bread', hundreds of words for 'woman' and 'apple'. For every necessary thing, there is a word in every language—a word that has been in the language for a long time, so I would guess. A chicken is a necessary thing. A man is necessary. A woman is necessary. An apple is necessary. Then there are the unnecessary things, like 'political party' and 'gun' and 'bomb'. Isn't it strange that the unnecessary things are the most dangerous? Well, except for 'woman'. A woman is necessary, but also dangerous in certain ways. When they lose their temper, they are dangerous. My wife can be dangerous sometimes. But very beautiful, too, even when she is dangerous.

While I am thinking of words and families, I think of the story told by Muslims of the way in which languages came to be. The story—a very old story—tells us that all the peoples of the world used to speak only one language and belonged to one family, but then some people—probably politicians—began to use the language to say that men were greater than God. And God took away their language for punishment, and people had to make up their own languages, many different languages, and so one part of the family could not understand the other. That is what happens with gifts from God. We use the gifts in the wrong way, and we lose them.

I find some friends playing cards and I decide to sit and join the game to pass the time. There is no television in November, no radio, no DVDs, no videos. Why this should be, I don't know. Maybe the authorities think that they would be rewarding us if they let us watch television. Maybe they think we would be too comfortable and that we would send secret messages back to our homelands and say to our relatives and friends, 'Come to Australia! Sell your house, borrow all the money you can! Sell your cows and goats and sheep and chickens. Sell your fruit trees. For in Australia they put you in a camp and let you watch television!'

I don't know. But at least we can play cards. We can sit together and let the sun move in the sky and tell stories as we play. The game we most often play is Fis kut. It is a game of the Middle East, for four players. If there are only two players, we play Farsool, another game of my country and the countries nearby. We never play for money. We are all gamblers, as I have said, but we only gamble with our lives, not with money. In any case, we have no money. Those who still had a few American dollars left when they reached Australia have surrendered them to the Australian Government.

Arguments start when we play Biscot. One player makes a mistake, and another player growls. There is nothing at stake, but still there are arguments. All of us in November, even the children, are on edge. We don't know what is going to happen. If we knew that we would have our cases decided in one month or two months or even in six months, probably we would all relax a bit, but because we don't know, every day is full of tension. It's just human to be anxious when you don't know what is to become of you. Sometimes funny ideas get into your head and you become a bit mad. You think that the authorities really know what your fate is to be, but they won't tell you. It's not true, but you can start believing things like that. Playing Biscot, you think to yourself, 'That stupid Hassan is not paying attention,' and you say, 'Hey, Hassan, keep your mind on the game.'

And Hassan says, 'What the hell are you talking about? I don't need some donkey from the hills getting clever with me.'

Next thing, you're shouting. I know when I'm anxious and short-tempered, and I keep myself under control. Not everybody can do that. Some of the people have had a harder journey than me. Some of the men have wives and children with them in the camp. The wife says to her husband, 'Make them tell us when we can leave this place. Tell them to hurry. The kids are going crazy.'

The husband can't make the authorities hurry, probably he wishes he could. So he gets into a bad mood, and maybe there's a fight, maybe somebody hits somebody else with a weapon, a piece of wood, something like that. The guards put you in another camp if you are violent—in Sierra, also part of Woomera. I feel sorry for some of the men who end up in Sierra; others, I think, 'Better you go to Sierra before you kill someone.'

The worst fights are not about cards or food or anything like that; the worst fights are about your country, where you come from. I'm from Afghanistan and I'm Hazara, so I always feel closer to the other Hazara from Afghanistan. We know the same things, we feel the same way. But I'm not stupid enough to think that the only good people are Hazara from Afghanistan. Every country has its good and bad; every tribe, too. Even though I know this, if somebody from another place says, 'All Hazara are donkeys!' something inside me gets angry.

I know from the way the officials and the guards shake their heads that they think we are hopeless, sometimes. We come all this way at the risk of our lives to find Australia, then one man punches another man in the head, and friends on both sides join in and before long, people have been sent to Sierra. If it is hard to make Australia want us when we are peaceful, how much harder is it when we are not? But the officials and the guards don't understand that when you live behind big fences, each day makes you more desperate. Anger and sorrow build up and build up, and good sense begins to starve to death. The people who keep us in November are not cruel, but often they don't see that the poem each man and each woman and each child carries inside is being forgotten. One day, the poem is no longer there. People forget how to be happy. People even forget how to be sad. They forget how to feel anything. If they get angry, they welcome it because at least they are feeling something.

After the card game, I wander about again. At this time of the day, my mind begins to go to sleep even while I walk about. I stop and look at a bird sitting on the fence, then I realise I have been standing and watching for 15 minutes. No thoughts come into my mind as I watch. My thoughts for today are used up.

I need something in my brain or I will become a ghost. It has already happened to some of the people here in November. When I see such a man I think, 'Would he bleed if he was cut? Has his blood disappeared from his veins?' The ghosts sit on their beds and stare at nothing. When you look into their eyes, you see only emptiness, like a room from which all the furniture has been removed.

I whistle for a few minutes. It is not a song I am whistling, just a sound. How long until dinner in the mess? Still two hours?

Where are my great plans, my daydreams? I must find my daydreams, just one of them will be enough. But not a sad daydream. A happy daydream.

Think, Najaf, think!

A car. That is one of my dreams. A car to drive in the big cities of Australia. Maybe a Toyota, six cylinders. Or a van. A van would be good. If it is to be a van, then it should be a Nissan. Excellent for carrying goods about. Excellent for carrying rugs. I notice a lot of traffic lights in Australia—more than in Mazar-e-Sharif. What is the orange light? Who knows, it doesn't matter. Red, stop; green, go—simple. The roads are smooth. I have seen them in Darwin. In Australia, I drive on only one side of the road. The Right side? Left? What is it? I will discover it one day in my life.

Another dream is a shop where I can sell rugs. Mazars, Solemanis, Saraks, Jamuds, Heratis; also Turkmans—Ersari, Saryk, Salun, Tekke. I offer my customers a cup of tea, then we look at the rugs. I have hundreds. I speak of the quality of the wool, and how tight the weave is in a true Afghan rug, and I speak of the dyes, all natural dyes using walnuts, pomegranates, flowers, onions. I show the customers the Bukhara design.

'This is the most important design in Afghan rugs—the Bukhara, the elephant footprint. It's very old. You see how it is repeated down the length of the rug? Very beautiful. Feel the surface with your hand. Run your palm along the nap. This is the best wool on earth for rugs—the best.'

It is dangerous to think about rugs; dangerous because I could get too sad to stand on my feet. But I do it anyway.

I go to the kitchen and the mess hall to prepare for the evening meal, which is usually the same as the midday meal: rice, chicken or beef, bread, tea. As the people come in, they make a queue at the serving counter—one of those famous queues that all of us jumped when we came to Australia. Except here, in the mess hall, there is no queue-jumping. Everybody has to wait in line and be well behaved. I am learning more about queues. As soon as I reached Australia, my education began. If I ever go back to Afghanistan, I will start a school and teach everyone about queues.

At the end of the day, the faces of the mothers and fathers all wear frowns. Another day has passed and nothing has happened. The children will be asking the same questions they have asked for weeks and months, 'When can we go to a house? When can we go to school?'

And the mothers and fathers will say, 'We don't know. We must wait.'

I think to myself as I serve the evening meal that all of us have been waiting in different places for such a long time that our waiting muscles are aching and sore. We waited in hiding while vans and cars carried us slowly across Afghanistan and Pakistan. We waited in Karachi for an aeroplane to take us to Jakarta. We waited in Jakarta for a people smuggler to find a boat. (And such a boat! Aiee!) We waited on the boat through heat and cyclones while the boat crossed the Timor Sea. We waited at Ashmore Reef for rescue. We waited for the Australian Navy after an aeroplane spotted us. We waited in Darwin for the authorities to look at our documents. And we wait here for the man at the big desk in the city of Canberra to put a tick or a cross or a question mark on our forms.

And I think of something else, too. I think that all of our waiting and our need for patience is caused by people who would not be patient and would not wait. I mean the people who did not wait before they dropped bombs on us, and did not wait before they fired rockets, and did not wait for the United Nations to make peace in our lands. Whenever people are impatient and will not wait, you can be sure there will be a cost. Big costs and small costs. My left shoe is one of the small costs.

4

Lambs and Wolves

MY FATHER DIED when I was still a small boy, although I cannot say exactly what age I was when I saw his body being laid out and washed. As I have already mentioned, we are not a nation of people who rely on documents. I would estimate that I was around eight years old, and the year in the Western calendar was 1979.

In the last days of that year, the Soviet Union leaders in Moscow decided to invade Afghanistan and install a man called Babrak Karmal to be the leader of our country. Karmal then 'invited' an enormous host of Soviet troops into Afghanistan to make sure he remained President. My father's death marked the commencement of decades of deaths in Afghanistan, not many of them as peaceful as his had been. Do you know that over the 20 years between 1979 and 1999, the life expectancy of both Afghani men and women fell, and so did the figure that measures the percentage of children surviving until their fifth birthday?

Watching the preparation of my father's body through a small crack in the wooden door of our farmhouse, I had no idea of the storm that was about to break over my country; no sense of dread. The foreboding I spoke of on the day of the rockets didn't stir in me in the least. Truly, the emotion I felt at that time was mostly one of curiosity, not even of grief. My father's limbs, which looked the same as in life, had to be lifted by those bathing him; his head was turned a little this way, then that way while his neck was washed. It was my father, but the strength, every last bit of it, had departed from his body. That is what I noticed. But sorrow? No, I did not feel true sorrow, but instead an acceptance. My father had ended his journey in life. It will sound strange, even a little callous for me to admit such a thing, but I have to point out that the childhood of an Afghani boy is not like that of a child in most Western countries. Afghani fathers are not sentimental; they practise a type of 'tough love', rearing their sons to face the hardships of life. For hardship has been a big part of the pattern of life in my violent homeland for not hundreds, but thousands of years.

Just look at the location of Afghanistan on a map of Asia and the Middle East, with neighbours and near-neighbours like Russia, Pakistan and Iran. Thousands of years ago, the Persians ruled Afghanistan (although it wasn't known then by that name), then the Macedonians of Alexander took the land from the Persians, followed by the Mongols and a whole host of tribal warriors from all over Central Asia. The British in India always wanted to make Afghanistan a secure neighbour, without any success at all; the Russians wanted an Afghanistan friendly to Moscow. And at various times, almost every tribal

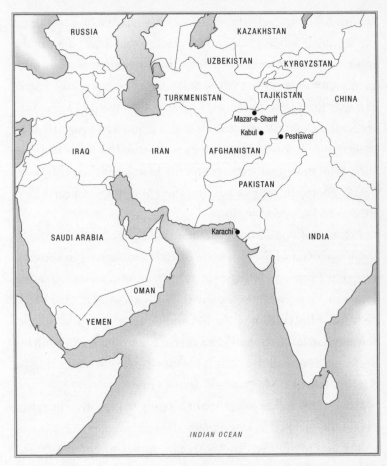

Afghanistan and surrounding countries

and ethnic group in the region has staked out its own little piece of the country. Afghanistan was not even recognised as a country in its own right until 1919; before that, it was simply a vast tract of valleys, mountains, deserts and plains that was supposed to fit into the political strategies of the powerful. Not that the powerful have ever listened to common sense, but if they had, any Afghani could have told them that it was not possible to conquer and subdue Afghanistan for more than a few years at a time. Amongst the four main ethnic groups of the country you'll find some of the most shrewd and fierce guerrilla fighters anywhere in the world. I am not a warrior; I don't like guns, I don't like explosions, I don't like war. But I have seen men, Afghanis, who would be prepared if necessary to commit themselves and a hundred generations of their family to battle, from now until the end of the world. For such men, individual honour and the honour of their tribe is so deeply rooted in their hearts that there is nothing on earth that they would not do to preserve it.

Let me tell you of one of the mujahedin leaders who fought the Russians and the Russian-backed communists in the civil war that I just barely survived. This man was wounded in the face in a battle with the Russians; badly wounded. One of his eyes was blown from its socket and dangled down his cheek. Rather than leave the battle, he cut the eye from his face with his knife and resumed the fight. This man is not unusual amongst Afghani fighters. Many would do the same.

An Afghani father has failed in his duty to his sons if he raises dreamers. He will have done his sons no favours. This is not to say that my father, or any Afghani father, attempts to force a brutal outlook on life on his sons. Not at all. Sons are loved; sons are a source of pride. My father loved me, but always with a view to the man I would become; always with attention to the things that would form the adult Najaf. That was his duty. The relationship of father and son in Afghanistan reaches maturity when the son becomes a man and displays to the father's satisfaction the qualities of fortitude, resourcefulness, loyalty and endurance that were impressed on him as a child. In the West, parents strive to make a paradise for their children to inhabit; to shield them from the reality of life; to shower them with joys and delights. In Afghanistan, the childhood of a boy is a time of testing.

The death of my father was not a personal catastrophe for me. I could expect to be cared for by my family. Indeed, I would not even be fatherless; my brother Gorg Ali would take over the role of father. Afghanis are a tribal people; the family is a smaller version of the tribe. It is expected that the eldest son will inherit the role of father to the family. It was my good fortune that I had older brothers, and my special good fortune that Gorg Ali was there to help raise me. He was a good man, wise and kind. Although I have said that Afghani fathers are rarely gentle, I have to confess that I am an Afghani son who enjoys gentleness. Gorg Ali was gentle.

I cannot recall exactly, but I believe that as I watched the preparation of my father's body, I would have been aware that Gorg Ali was now the most important person in my life. It would have been important to me to know that. In a way, having Gorg Ali allowed me to watch the washing of my father's limbs, the turning of his body, the arrangement of his hands without distress. My father would go into the earth and his spirit would be taken up to Heaven. My life would go on as it had. I would continue to tend the lambs in the hill pastures. I would continue to return in the late afternoon to my home in the village of Shar Shar. My mother would be waiting. Abdul Ali, my second-oldest brother, would greet me in his unsmiling and severe way. But Gorg Ali would place his hand on my shoulder and ask me quietly if the lambs were safe.

Keeping the lambs safe was my first occupation. I can truthfully say that I am a shepherd by trade, although rugs now mean more to me than sheep. From a young age, it was my task each day to gather the lambs of our flock, perhaps 40 or 50 of them, and lead them to the hill pastures for the day. There, they would graze on the high grass while I watched patiently. In the early morning when it was barely light, I would move from foot to foot to prevent the cold from getting into my bones. Sometimes the ground was covered by a fall of snow and the temperature close to freezing. At such times, I pulled my coat close to my body and imagined the warmth of my home awaiting me later in the day. The cold was often so fierce and the air so dry that the skin of my hands and heels would split. When that happened, it was necessary to rub mutton fat into the flesh to moisten it, otherwise the openings in the skin would grow wider and deeper and become too painful to bear. Another way of treating split skin was to gather the small pellets of gum from the spiky Khar plant, then chew the gum to soften it, smear it on the broken flesh and light it, so that the melted gum sealed the cracks. Remedies such as this were known to all Afghanis, and not only for broken flesh but for countless other ailments. I grew up understanding the properties of the herbs and plants all around me. When you know what to look for, a mountainside becomes a pharmacy.

Watching lambs as they grazed was not just a matter of staying awake. The lambs were important to the survival of my family. If I lost a single lamb through daydreaming or dozing, it would bring trouble down on my head. I had to make sure that they were not stolen or taken by the wolves of the mountains. I would have been no match for a wolf but I had a big dog with me, and no wolf was a match for him.

When I recall the years of my childhood roaming the

mountainside and counting the lambs, I think of peace. The beauty of the countryside around Shar Shar comes back to me with great force. I think of the silence, and of the mists and clouds and the sunshine and the snow and how bright the grass was in spring. I find myself yearning for peace of that sort, and to live all day at such a quiet pace. What did I have to trouble me? I was doing my job, the dog was doing his job, the lambs were growing fatter and taller. And so it is a paradise that I bring to mind; a blessed place. But the truth is that I did not think of my mountainside as a paradise at the time. No, not at all. I dreamed of visiting the city, Mazar-e-Sharif. I dreamed of motor cars speeding down the streets, and of shops full of things to buy, and of people shouting and jostling, and of the great Mosque of Mazar-e-Sharif and of the shrine of Ali. I had seen Mazar-e-Sharif briefly when my family made a visit, travelling by open van over the dusty roads. I wanted to see more of it.

In the middle of the day, I sat in the grass above the lambs and ate my lunch. My brother Gorg Ali was a beekeeper (one of his many trades) and our household always had honey for bread and cooking. My lunch was a narrow, flattened loaf of bread full of honey. I kept it all through the morning wrapped tightly in a cloth and when I unfolded the cloth the bread was rich with the honey that had soaked into it. I ate it greedily gazing down at the lambs or watching the hawks turning slow, wide circles in the sky.

My dog had to watch the sheep more closely than ever while I ate. He knew this. He knew he had to wait until late afternoon for his next meal. But even so, he hoped, not always in vain, for a scrap of my bread and honey. He was good company—his name would translate into English as, 'Hey, you!'—it's not the custom in Afghanistan to give a special name to a dog or cat, or to any animal. I carried out my duty to the sheep, and the dog carried out his duty to me.

I carried a bottle of water with me, and once my bread and honey was gone, I swallowed down a mouthful of water. What lay before me was all that I understood of life and of the world.

Or would it be true to say that all I understood of the world was what I could see when I watched the lambs? No, probably not, for I also went to school off and on in the summer months and learned a little about the bigger world around me. But what I learnt went in one ear and out the other. I was not an attentive student. Compared to the real work of living, schooling seemed to me an absurd waste of time. How could it help me to know of the great oceans of the world, of the continents, of lands ten thousand miles away that I would never visit? Mathematics—yes, I could see a use for mathematics, for counting, for measuring. And to know a little of the history of my country did no harm either. To know how to read and write—yes, there was some point to that. Well, when I think of it, there was some point to almost everything I was taught in school, yes. But our teacher was a hard, unsmiling man so ready to use his fists or the length of wood he always kept within his reach. How could I, or any of the boys in the school, enjoy being his captive for the whole day? I suppose he was thought to have the right sort of temperament for teaching. In Afghanistan, all teachers go about their job in the same way, boxing the ears of boys who smile at the wrong time, or even at the right time. My teacher wasn't sadistic or cruel, I wouldn't say that of him. But boxing ears was his first duty and he never forgot it.

What was it about me that so attracted his blows? I was a cheerful boy, so maybe it was my smiles and my laughter. He must have thought that I wasn't taking schooling seriously. Sometimes I got fed up with him and ran away at lunchtime. I recall sitting at my desk one morning with my exercise book open on the armrest thinking of all the outside places I preferred to the classroom. I could see the houses of Shar Shar and the pastures beyond them. I thought of the sun on my face and of having no one to please but the lambs on the hillside. I had already been treated to three or four blows from the teacher that morning and I didn't want any more. At lunchtime, I wandered away to the open pastures at the back of the school. I had my sandwich with me and when I thought I was concealed from the teacher's gaze, I lay down in the grass by a stream and ate the sandwich and rejoiced in my freedom. When I was thirsty, I flattened myself on the grass and drank from a stream. I was full of delight at my own daring. 'Who has the brains to outwit Najaf?' I thought. 'No one! Najaf comes and goes as he pleases!'

Then I heard the voice of my teacher. 'You drink like a donkey,' he said.

He grabbed me by the neck and dragged me back to the classroom. I sat for the rest of the day imagining a world in which teachers were prisoners of the pupils. But I was also a little in awe of my teacher's skill in tracking me down. How had he known where to look for me? It seemed like witchcraft.

The teacher wasn't all that interested in education himself, in all honesty. Once we were left in his care, he was free to do what he liked with us. Often he would despatch us like household slaves to do chores for him or for his wife.

'Najaf Mazari, off to the pastures, gather gum for my wife and take it to her.'

The gum was used for protecting the skin against cracking in the cold, as I have explained. I resented being sent on chores for the teacher and his wife. Children all over the world, even those in harsh countries like my own, have such a powerful sense of justice and injustice. I knew it was wrong of my teacher to make me his servant. But what could be done? My brother Gorg Ali had no sympathy for my complaints, nor for any truancy. As I gathered the gum from the Khar plants, I imagined diabolical punishments being inflicted on my teacher. Let him be captured by a devil and made to spend his days gathering gum all over Afghanistan! May he be deprived of sleep at night and fed on stale bread without honey! May the water he drinks be full of silt! And may he be made to begin his chores again at the break of day!

School was misery for me, that's true, but I must confess that life was easier for me than for many of my classmates. I had an exercise book to write in, at least. I had a sandwich to eat at lunchtime. I had a warm house to return to in cold weather. Others had fewer comforts. Sometimes the teacher would take us outdoors in the hot weather and make us sit in a circle on the ground. The boys who had no exercise books had to write their lessons in the white dust with their fingers.

I did not attend school each day of the week. That was not the way of things in an Afghan village. All boys of my age had tasks to complete each day, and school had to fit around those tasks. The lambs came first, school came second. The compulsory education of Western countries was still a long way off in the Afghanistan of my boyhood, and it remains as far off as ever. And there was more to occupy boys of my age than tasks, for in the winter months, we all attended Koranic classes at the mosque. The resentment I felt at being forced to sit at a desk in primary school never found its way into my heart at Koranic classes, not because the mosque school was enjoyable or exciting, but because it would have been a terrible sin to feel such resentment. The mullah who taught us made sure that we knew where Hell was, and what it was like, and what sort of people were likely to end up there. The impious were certainly bound for Hell. The mullah spoke of eternal punishment in the flames, and of the screams of the wicked as they begged for forgiveness.

'Will they find forgiveness, the wicked ones?' the mullah asked. 'No, they will not find forgiveness. Their punishment will never end. Woe to anyone who passes through the gates of Hell!'

* * *

With the reader's permission, I will make a great leap through time and over distance at this point in my story, just for a minute or two. This is the adult Najaf talking; Najaf who has to shave each morning, and earn a living for his family; who has to struggle with the GST and Business Activity Statements. I am not in Shar Shar at this moment; I am not even in Afghanistan. I am in Australia, standing outside a primary school, a government school in Windsor in the state of Victoria. I can see through the windows of the school. I can see the lady teacher talking to her class. My daughter Maria is in that class. On the walls of the classroom the teacher and the pupils have hung their pictures and paintings. It is a bright room, full of colour. And full of noise too—the noise of children chattering happily like a flock of birds. I can hear the chatter from where I stand. Now the teacher raises her voice a little and claps her hands and the pupils become quiet and sit up straight at the tables. The teacher has something to say to the class. All the pupils listen closely. The teacher must be telling the children what she has in store for them this morning; what lessons she has planned. She is smiling. Whatever she has to say pleases the children, I can see that. The day's lessons are about to begin. Maria, with her shining black hair, catches a glimpse of me standing outside. She gives me a smile and a wave, then begins to busy herself with her exercise book and her pencils.

5

The Room of Questions

THE ROOM AT WOOMERA where case officers interview
people like me is very plain. A door opens into the room from
the outside, and a second door opens at the back from another
office. It is a small room with bare walls, just big enough for
three or four people to sit and talk. A wooden desk stands on the
dark carpet almost in the centre of the room, with one of those
swivelling chairs at the back for the case officer and three chairs
with fixed legs facing him: one for the person being interviewed;
one for a lawyer or a representative; and one for an interpreter.
It is a room where questions are asked—suspicious questions,
friendly questions, clever questions, a few stupid questions.
And it is a room where answers are given to those questions—
suspicious answers, friendly answers, clever answers, and a few
stupid answers. A very plain room, as I say, but God knows
how much heartache and pain and despair and sometimes joy

those bare walls have witnessed. In this room, hope comes up like the sun, or sinks behind the mountains forever.

At this, my third interview in Woomera, I enter that room with my heart pounding like a drum, although I try to look as calm as I can. Even people who have nothing to hide and intend to tell the whole truth to the case officer become nervous when they enter the interview room. I think to myself, 'But what if the Australians have asked questions in Shar Shar or in Mazar-e-Sharif and somebody who hates me or my family has told them lies? What if somebody has said that I am a rogue or a bandit, just to make mischief?' I try to think of people who might make mischief in this way, but it seems to me there is no one. We are not a rich family, so there could be no envy. We don't gossip. My father had been a respected man, and Gorg Ali, too; everyone in Shar Shar and Mazar-e-Sharif considered Gorg Ali a man of honour. Maybe my younger brother Rosal Ali had made enemies when he was alive. That was easy to imagine. He'd made enemies inside his own family with his easy-come, easy-go ways. But really, the poor child has been dead for 17 years, and in any case, who would harbour a grudge against Rosal Ali, who did no harm to anyone except himself?

While I am waiting anxiously for my third interview, I begin to think about truth and lies. I will be telling the truth when I speak with the case officer, but he would surely have heard some lies in his job. It is not that people mean to lie to case officers; it is just that the truth is sometimes so complicated, and so sometimes people try to make it simpler to accept. I'll tell you what I mean. Let's say that the Taliban has been trying to kill a certain man, and to save himself, he goes about saying nice things about the Taliban—about how kind and generous and God-fearing they are, nonsense like that—because he hopes that the Taliban will hear some of the nice things he's saying and will decide to leave him alone. And what if the Australians should make some enquiries in his town and learn that the man has said nice things about the Taliban? Maybe the truth is that even after saying nice things about the Taliban, they still wanted to kill the man; maybe his plan was all a waste of time. This is hard to explain so the man might tell the case officer that he came from a village that is not his real village. It is a lie, but it is a lie that helps tell the bigger truth.

For me, I have no need to tell lies of any sort, even those that serve the truth. The Taliban really did want to kill me, and I never thought of any plan that would stop them, except for the plan of getting out of Afghanistan altogether. And I am glad that I can tell the truth, for lies are a form of theft; the liar steals from another person that person's trust. There are liars all over the world who have grown rich on the trust they have stolen.

For this interview, as for my others, I am assisted by an interpreter. I have been picking up little bits and pieces of English, but not nearly enough for an important interview. The interpreter is an Afghani, older than me. I am only supposed to know him by a number, but I happen to know that his name is Amin. And for this interview, I have a representative who assists the Afghanis in detention centres such as Woomera. His name is Petra.

We enter the interview room together and wait for the case officer to appear before we sit down. I stand with my hands at my sides, trying to look happy. Amin chats with me, telling me to relax.

'Take it easy,' he says. 'This guy will just ask you a few questions. No problem.'

The door opens at the back of the room and the case officer steps in with cardboard folders in his hand and a tape recorder. He smiles at us, and waves at the chairs, inviting us to sit down. He seems friendly straight away. I like him. He's a man of about 50 with a beard turning grey, a little bit bald on top of his head. He wears neat trousers and a white shirt. The first thing he does is to turn on his tape recorder and place it on the side of the desk, close to me. Then he says something or the other; the date and the time, I think. When he looks across the desk at Amin and at Petra and me, his eyes sparkle behind his glasses. He says something to Amin, then looks at me while Amin interprets his words.

'His name is Robert,' says Amin. 'He says you can call him Bob.'

'Why do I call him Bob if his name is Robert?' I ask. I am puzzled.

'Who knows? That's what he says. Just call him Bob, don't worry about it.'

'Bob?'

'Yes, Bob.'

'It's a funny name.'

'It's an Australian name. Don't make a big deal of it. Just call him Bob.'

'Okay. Bobah? Is that how you say it?'

'No. Say, "Bo-*b*".'

'Bo-*b*?'

'Close enough.'

Bob seems to know what Amin is saying. He smiles and opens his cardboard folders and spreads some papers on the desk. I glance down at them. Some of them, I've seen before.

Bob writes on the paper label of a cassette tape then fits it into the player and turns it on. He says a few things I can only partly follow, and Amin doesn't bother to translate at this stage. I make out the word, 'Woomera' and the date. Then Amin begins to translate:

'His name is Bob Johnson, he's an officer of the Department of Immigration. Your name is Najaf Mazari and your nationality is Afghani. I am a registered translator with the Department within the meaning of the Act. I am sworn to speak to no one at all other than to Mr Johnson himself of the discussions in this room. Nothing you say to Mr Johnson will be repeated in any form to authorities in Afghanistan. Okay?'

'Okay,' I say.

Mr Johnson has something else to say that takes up more than a minute. It sounds very serious to me, and I'm worried about it. Maybe he's saying to Amin, 'We are going to throw this man into prison.' But when Amin translates, it's all to do with penalties for telling lies, and I know that I won't be telling lies so I relax and say, 'That's okay.'

Then Mr Johnson tells me through Amin of all the people who would be allowed to read what I was saying—people in the Government of Australia and people in the police force and Australians who want to make enquiries about me in Afghanistan. By the time Mr Johnson has finished telling me of all the people in the world who will be permitted to read my words, I'm beginning to feel that I might as well tell my whole story in the newspaper. But I don't say that. I just say, 'Sure.'

'Now he wants to know where you came from,' says Amin.

'Where I come from? Mazar-e-Sharif.' What a crazy question. It's written right there on the documents in front of Mr Johnson.

'And is Mazar-e-Sharif a small town or a big town or a small city or a big city?'

Crazier and crazier.

'It's a big city,' I say. Then I think of the Australian cities I've seen and those I've heard about, such as Sydney, which is so big that its buildings crowd each other out and people have to build higher and higher into the air. I say, 'In Afghanistan, it's big. Here, maybe not so big.'

'And what famous buildings are found in the city of Mazar-e-Sharif?'

Okay, I'm beginning to get it now. Mr Johnson is giving me a test. Why doesn't he just say so? He can ask me anything. I know the names of half of the shops in Mazar-e-Sharif. I can tell him where I bought Coca-Cola, and where I bought bread, and where my friends and I used to buy sweets when we had a little bit of money, and where we played cops-and-robbers— everything.

'Lots of famous buildings,' I say. 'The hospital. The government buildings where all the offices are kept. The police barracks. The bazaar, many famous buildings around the bazaar.'

'One building is very famous.'

'Very famous?' I try to think. Is this a trick? What does he mean when he says, 'very famous'? I look at the representative, Petra, but he just shrugs.

'Very famous in what way?'

'A very famous shrine.'

'Oh! Okay, now I know what you mean. The Shrine of Ali.'

The problem was that we Afghanis don't think of a mosque as a famous place. Somebody coming to Mazar-e-Sharif to visit the Shrine of Ali would not say, 'Can you tell me where the famous Shrine of Ali is to be found?' He would say, 'Where is the Holy Shrine of Ali?' If something is holy, we don't call it famous, because it is too holy to be famous.

Mr Johnson asks me about my mother and my father and my brothers and my uncles and my aunts and my cousins. He asks me about Shar Shar, and about school, and about being a shepherd in the mountains. He asks me what sort of food my mother made for us. He asks me what sort of work I did in Mazar-e-Sharif, and about the work my brothers did, and about our house in Mazar-e-Sharif, and what the house was made of, and about the seasons and the flowers that grew around Mazar-e-Sharif, and the fruits that could be purchased in the markets and the rugs that could be purchased in the bazaar. After a while, it feels as if I am having a conversation with Mr Johnson. I almost forget about Amin and Petra. I answer every question as well as I can, and sometimes I add extra information just because it's enjoyable to speak about my homeland and my family.

Only once do I become upset, and that's when Mr Johnson asks me about Gorg Ali, and how he died. Speaking about Gorg Ali makes me cry, for I can see him in my mind standing beside me with his hand on my shoulder, me only a small boy. I think of him on the day he went back to Shar Shar to tend to the hives of the bees, and I think of the gun being fired from somewhere that sends the bullet through the air and through his body and kills him. Speaking of Gorg Ali makes me think all over again of how much I had loved this good man. Why should anyone wish to kill Gorg Ali? To make a good man, God has to use all of his skill. Some of the goodness of God himself goes into such a man. And when the man is made and is ready to take his place on the earth, God must feel the pride that I feel when I look at the rug I am weaving, at the strands that bind closely together and knot and make a pattern, and at the beauty of the colours. Such a long day's work to make a good man! And yet, one bullet that takes a second to speed through the air and strike a man will kill him in an instant. How can God forgive such a thing? And yet He can, so it is said, for His heart is great and His forgiveness infinite, if the sinner repents. But I am not God and I cannot forgive the man who killed my brother. It makes me weep, as it does this day, right before Mr Johnson.

When the interview is finished, I don't know whether I have made a good impression. Maybe. Mr Johnson remains friendly all the way through the interview, but he is probably like that with everyone. I go back to the dormitory and think over all I have said. If it was my job to let people into a country, I would let me in. Why not? Australia needs more Afghanis. We work hard all day long. We sing, sometimes. We make beautiful rugs. Also, we don't complain very often. Why should we? In Mazar-e-Sharif and Kabul and Kandahar, people shoot you. Here, nobody shoots you. I heard that the government took all the guns away from people who had guns. A good thing. I agree with taking guns away from people. What can you make with a gun? Can you make a rug with a gun? Can you build a family with a gun? Can you show your love for your wife with a gun, your love for your daughter? No. A gun has one purpose, and that purpose will not build anything, but will only tear down what others have built.

6

Kisses

MY FATHER'S DEATH meant that my older brothers Gorg Ali and Abdul Ali were free to make their own plans for the future of our family. While my father was alive, his word was law. Although he would listen to advice and often accept it from his elder sons, it was understood that my father had the final say in all important matters. This was not just the custom within my family, but throughout Afghanistan. The father is the chieftain of his small tribe. As Muslims, Afghanis believe that this arrangement is as God intended. But I must tell you that within Afghani families, women are not powerless. They are not puppets that are made to do this and that and the other, whether it suits them or not. The husband will decide where the family's house is to be built and of what material it is to be built, but the wife rules the inside of the house. Also, the wife will influence her husband in many ways. Decisions that appear to have come entirely from the mind and mouth of the husband have often been fashioned by the will of the wife.

In the matter of where the family's house would stand, my father and mother had the same opinion. It should stand in Shar Shar. That was the place on earth that my father and mother knew best. My brother Gorg Ali had bigger plans, and once he took over as head of the family, he turned his gaze to the north, to the city of Mazar-e-Sharif, and so it came about that our family left Shar Shar and began a new life in Mazar-e-Sharif. So far as I was concerned, this move to a new place on the earth suited me well. Looking after sheep is a fine job for a time, but it was not truly what I was born to. What it was that I was born to I didn't know, but a voice in my heart told me that I would find it in Mazar-e-Sharif.

I played a small part in the construction of the new house, but at least that small part allowed me to mix my sweat with the earth that was fashioned to make the walls and roof of the house, and so I earned the right to call this place my home. It is important to Afghanis to feel that what comforts come from God have been earned, and this is particularly important to the Hazara. We are a people who have never known great luxury, and in any case, we do not trust it. I will tell you a story of the great leader and champion of the Hazara in modern times. He was a man cut out to be a leader. He fought all those who wished to make the Hazara a vassal class within Afghanistan, the Taliban in particular. It was Abdul Ali Mazari who inflicted on the Taliban the rare defeats in their campaign to rule Afghanistan. All that Abdul Ali Mazari asked of the Taliban was for Hazara representation in whatever government they formed according to the percentage of the Hazara in the overall population of Afghanistan, which is around 20 per cent. The Taliban commanders agreed to negotiate with Abdul Ali, but the negotiations ended in his murder. The Taliban went to Abdul Ali's home even before his body had cooled, expecting to seize all the wealth and goods he had accumulated over the years as a great lord of the Hazara. They found a dwelling as simple as that of a farmer. They searched for the gold he must have hidden away beneath the house or in the fields, but found nothing because there was nothing to find. Abdul Ali had lived in no greater splendour than the poorest of the people he ruled.

In Afghanistan, the main building material for houses is the earth on which the house is to stand. The earth is packed into wooden forms to make regular mud bricks, or into slab moulds to make larger bricks. The earth is mixed with grasses of two sorts, depending on the thickness of the brick. Almost every boy in Afghanistan above a certain age knows how to make mud bricks, as I did by the age of 12 when we were preparing to move to Mazar-e-Sharif. My contribution to the building of the house was to mix the mud and grass of the brick, packing the moulds and taking the dried bricks from their wooden moulds to Abdul Ali and Gorg Ali. They were more skilled, and had charge of laying the bricks.

It was the construction of the roof that gave me the greatest chance to assist. The roof of an Afghan house is made in a way that I'm sure was the same thousands of years ago. First, a long beam is fixed along the highest point of the house, then a framework of spars is joined to the roof beam, followed by a grid of narrower spars fixed close enough together to support the mud bricks. A layer of Borya grass is carefully spread over the framework, then a layer of mud bricks is laid on the Borya.

A layer of insulating grass covers the mud bricks, and a thinner surface of mud tiles finishes the roof. There is great craft in making the roof, and it will last forever if it is made well, or unless a rocket comes down in the night and smashes into it, which was to be the fate of this roof. I worked with pride on the mud bricks and did not know what was to come, thank God. For who would wish to know the future? How does a man benefit by knowing what he cannot change? In any case, it is wrong to ask God what the future holds. Time belongs to Allah, and He will dispose of it as He wishes. Surely He will be impatient with those who ask about His plans.

When the house was made and my family had settled in, I looked around with excitement and joy. A city like Mazar-e-Sharif was as grand a place as New York or Paris to me. What might I accomplish here? What adventures might I have? In Shar Shar, the world stretched north, south, east and west. And past the line to which I could see, I expected more of the same: more mountains, more pastures, more sheep, more people like my teacher who boxed my ears for no reason, more snow to freeze my feet. In Mazar-e-Sharif, I thought that the world past where I could see must be full of wonders. It was one of those times in my life—it must be the same for everyone—when sunshine follows rain and seeds in the ground stretch up stalks and leaves to capture the warmth and grow bigger. In my body, I could feel the days of spring beginning, and I could feel the new season in my body, too. I thought more than ever of girls, of women, of how wonderful they were, how desirable.

A wedding was planned for my brother's friend Sayeed Assad, and it was first a rumour then a fact that I would be permitted to attend. A wedding in Afghanistan is a time of great rejoicing, and a time for the bride's family and the groom's family and friends to open their purses wide. No Afghani wishes to be mistaken for a miser at the time of his wedding. It is thought, 'Let everyone who remembers my wedding day bless the hours he spent in my house!' Weddings attract hundreds of guests and it is not unusual for the hundreds to become a thousand in the case of a very rich family. The numbers are so high because Afghanis are a tribal people, and those of your tribe must not be overlooked.

The day of Sayeed Assad's wedding began with a procession— of the bride's and groom's family members and closest friends— to the house of the bride's parents for the wedding service. Sayeed Assad that day wore the look that all Afghani men wear on their wedding day—a shy look, mixed with happiness and pleasure. This is the expected look, and the bride must appear even shyer than her husband-to-be. God is close on a wedding day, and He would not wish to see any boastful expressions.

I was too insignificant a person to be invited into the house of the bride's family for the wedding service, but I was able to glance in the door and see what was happening inside. In any case, I had been permitted to watch other weddings in the past, smaller than this one, and I knew exactly the way in which the service would unfold.

The mullah, who is also the principal guest on a wedding day, seats himself on the floor before the family members, with the bride and groom nearest to him, also seated on the floor in the Afghani manner. The mullah then offers a greeting to everyone in the name of God and the Prophet, and the guests and the bride and groom join in to bless the name of God and the name of the Prophet and all of the Prophet's progeny and ancestors. The mullah reads the groom's history aloud, telling all the members of the two families that since birth the groom has been a faithful servant of God and of the Prophet and, with his speech and actions, he has honoured the name of God and the Prophet throughout his life, and that he has prayed and fasted in accordance with the rituals of the Faith, and that he has remained chaste and holy in preparation for this day, when God and the Prophet are close. The mullah's story tells of the place where the groom was born, and into which family he was born, and whether he was the first or second or third or tenth child of that family. The mullah also tells of the deeds and piety of the groom's father and grandfather and great-grandfather and maybe even great-great-grandfather, and of the deeds and piety of the mother's family. Then the mullah speaks of the more day-to-day details of the groom's life: his hard work in this way or that way, his accomplishments in his work or his craft, his reliability, his honesty, his loyalty. The mullah pauses three times in his reading of the groom's history, and at each pause he asks the bride if she indeed wants to marry this man after having heard his history. And the bride says, 'Yes.'

The mullah then speaks of the bride's history, and of her family, and her deeds and accomplishments within her father's house, and of her skill in the preparation of food, her punctuality when setting meals on the table, her thrift in the marketplace, her eye for bargains, her cleanliness and good nature, her quiet voice and especially of the fact that she is slow to rouse to anger and would rather suffer a long, long time before complaining about anything. The mullah pauses three times in his telling of the bride's history and asks the groom if he indeed wants to marry this woman having heard her history. And the groom says, 'Yes.'

All through the service, each man watching keeps his hands raised before himself with the fingers parted, not high in the air but just a little way from the ground, and this shows that the groom has not touched the woman who is to be his bride. The groom wears a knot in the hem of his shirt where the two sides of the shirt join, and this shows that he has remained chaste.

Once Sayeed Assad's marriage service was concluded, the men within the house came out to greet all those who had gathered for the feasting and dancing and music. The women stayed inside for a time, as is the custom, then they too came out to join all the guests. It was evening by this time, for marriages are always held at the end of the day, after the men have returned from their work. In a field, rugs and kilims and sheets of plastic had been laid for the guests to sit on. Before the feasting and celebrations begin, a procession of cars and buses driven by guests and family members and friends of the bride and groom drove three times around the great shrine of Ali in Mazar-e-Sharif. Beggars came out and stopped the procession by holding knotted scarves across the road, and the guests and friends of the bride and groom had to offer money to the beggars before the procession was allowed to continue. This was expected, and money would be kept ready.

I was with three of my friends on this day of Sayeed Assad's wedding. For us, the biggest thrill of the day was not the ceremony or even the food and drink (although the food and drink were of course very important to us) but the dancing. A famous dancer was to perform at the wedding, a woman of renowned beauty and skill, and my three friends and I wanted to see as much of her as we possibly could. We had heard stories of her genius and had used these stories as the building blocks of dreams. We had no idea of how we would achieve more than watching her with hundreds of other guests, but as is the case with children, we trusted that we would think of something when the moment should come.

Afghani dancing is not a form of the dancing that people in the West see when they visit Middle Eastern restaurants and a girl with fair hair who is studying economics at the university performs what is known as a 'belly dance' to recorded music. This is not dancing. This is noise and movement. The dancing of Afghanistan is to belly dancing what a fine feast prepared by a master chef is to a hamburger from the restaurants of McDonald's. The finest women dancers of Afghanistan learn their craft from a very young age, and much of what they know when they reach womanhood cannot be taught unless the lessons begin in childhood. The dance tells a story, and the story must flow like the clear waters of a stream. When Afghanis watch a fine dancer, they pay attention to the movements of her hands and to the way she holds her head and how nimbly she moves her feet and how cleverly she uses the music of the musicians in the band. It is not a sex show, although the beauty of the dancer is certainly something that men remember.

At Sayeed Assad's wedding, daira, drums, rubab, tambor and tula made the music. The musicians sometimes put down one instrument and picked up another. All of these instruments—some strummed, some played across the strings with a bow, some like the tula (a pipe played by blowing into the mouthpiece)—require great skill in their use. The musicians and the dancer are both paid a lot of money when they perform at a wedding.

But before the dancing, came the eating and drinking. I sat with my friends and imitated what the adults were doing.

A huge urn of water was carried amongst the guests for the washing of hands. The water carrier had a brass jug which he filled from the urn, then poured over my hands. The person sitting next to me passed me a handtowel so that I could dry my hands and when I was done, I placed the towel on the shoulder of the person to my left. The food was served by waiters from big, silver trays, and nobody stopped you if you filled your plate as high as a mountain top. My friends and I fed ourselves as much as our stomachs would hold.

The night was kind to us; not hot, not too cold. The stars stood above us in the clear sky. The guests talked together and clapped the musicians and called for more food. Many people gathered together make a lot of noise, but the noise of the people at Sayeed Assad's wedding feast was a happy noise, with laughter mixed in, and many of the guests raising a hand toward the stars and calling to the heavens to bless the marriage of Sayeed Assad and his bride.

The dancer stepped into the broad space in the centre of the crowd of wedding guests, and the musicians played the music that Afghanis love. Even though the Talibs would one day take away the music and smash the instruments and beat the musicians, it was not possible for them to kill the love of music in the people. In that time of the Taliban which was still to come, many musicians hid their instruments away, burying them in the ground after wrapping them carefully. But on this day of Sayeed Assad's wedding feast, we did not know the future. We clapped loudly and called out compliments to the dancer who was so renowned, and men leapt onto the space where she was dancing and placed banknotes on her head to thank her for her performance. The dancer did not stop dancing when the money was placed on her head. The money fell to the ground, and one of the people who travelled with her and with the musicians hurried out to collect it.

What people had said about the beauty and skill of the dancer had not been exaggerated. I watched her in a dream, full of wonder at her movements. Her hands shaped the story she was telling from the dark of the night. Her long black hair seemed to me as beautiful as the black silk that is woven into rugs. Yes, I said her hair, the dancer's hair. In Afghanistan, dancers may perform with their hair uncovered, for the history of this dancing goes back to the time before the Prophet and before the rules of dress that we honour now. The dancing is older than all religions on earth, and so the dancer is permitted to show that time before Heaven came to be.

I will tell a story of the esteem that a great dancer enjoys in Afghanistan; a story that is known all over the country. It's the story of Kandhi Hazara, the most famous dancer in our history. This is exactly the way the story was told to me.

Kandhi Hazara came from a poor family of the Hazara and married a man who owned very little, as is the case with honest people, for the more honest a man is, the less he might own. But Kandhi Hazara had a great gift that was given to her perhaps by God Himself, who can say? One day, Kandhi Hazara's husband came home from working in the fields and saw that something was different in his house. He looked about, not knowing what it could be. Then he saw that a beautiful rug was spread on the floor. He asked his wife, 'How is this, that a rug of such beauty is found in my house?'

And his wife said, 'Well, don't question it, husband, it is a fine thing to look at.'

The husband came home another day and saw a second rug, as beautiful as the first, and also new cushions to rest on, and silver chalices to drink from. 'How can this be?' he asked his wife, as he had the first time, and Kandhi Hazara said, 'Don't concern yourself, husband, these are beautiful things for us to enjoy and to show our visitors.'

A third time the husband came home from the fields and saw even more rugs, all as fine as the ones that had so mysteriously appeared in his house in the past, and he saw many new plates for the serving of food. This time the husband was torn between rage and sorrow, and he said to his wife, 'How can this be? Such things are purchased with money, and the money I give you to buy food for the household is scarcely enough to feed us. Wife, I fear that you must be making money on the street, that is what I fear, God forgive you!'

Kandhi Hazara did not answer her husband, but she saw that something must be done to set his mind at rest. And so she went from the room for a short time, leaving her husband in despair, and when she returned she was dressed for dancing with her hair uncovered, and she danced before her husband. So in this way, he came to know her secret, and he forgave her trickery when he saw what skill she had.

Kandhi Hazara danced at weddings with her husband's permission (not that she had bothered with his permission in the past) and her grace in dancing was far greater than anyone could recall. She became famous all over Afghanistan, and commanded fees so high that it was no wonder that she and her husband became wealthy and moved to a new house with a high wall and the finest furnishings and a fountain in the centre of the courtyard. In the time of the communists, she was free to dance where she pleased, but those who hated the communists, the mujahedin, had no time for Kandhi Hazara, she who danced before men with her hair uncovered. It was decided by a mujahedin commander that Kandhi Hazara must die, and so the commander sent a soldier, who was trusted and brave and honoured God, to kill her at her house in the night. Amongst the mujahedin soldiers there was a man who had seen Kandhi Hazara dance and he honoured her greatly and could not stand by while she was killed. So he warned her of what was to come.

She said, 'Worry yourself no further, I will not run from any man and I will not leave my house.'

The soldier who admired Kandhi Hazara feared the worst when the assassin set out one night to kill her. But he needn't have troubled himself. When the assassin came to Kandhi Hazara's house, he struck the gates with his fist and demanded to be let in. The servant whose task it was to open the gates for visitors called in fear to his mistress, but she said, 'Open the gates wide.' And so he did. As soon as the assassin stepped into the courtyard, he saw Kandhi Hazara standing as still as a statue before him. Music began to play, and Kandhi Hazara danced. Her dancing was so graceful that the assassin lowered his gun and stared in wonder.

'It will not be by my hand that such a woman as this comes to grief,' he said, and returned to his commander in the hills. 'I saw her, but it won't be me who shoots her,' he said to his commander. The commander was amazed. The assassin he had sent was one of his best soldiers. So then he chose a second assassin, a soldier who obeyed every order on the battlefield without question and who would lay down his life for his commander without a sound. Once again, Kandhi Hazara was warned of what was to come, but she said, 'When he comes, the gates will be opened for him.' Sure enough, the assassin came in the night to kill her, and the gates were opened for him, and he saw Kandhi Hazara standing in the moonlight as still as a statue. His gun was ready, but he thought he would watch Kandhi Hazara dance before he shot her. She danced, and the assassin watched in wonder, then he shook his head and said to himself,

'Well, somebody may shoot this woman one day, but for what reason I do not know.' And he went back to his commander in the hills and told him that he had seen Kandhi Hazara and had taken a vow that it would not be by his hand that she would die.

The commander was not angry; not with the first soldier nor with the second. He saw that something strange was in the air when his soldiers watched Kandhi Hazara dance. He was wise enough not to trust himself to shoot her when soldiers so brave and obedient could not bring themselves to do so. He decided on a new plan, and went one night with four soldiers to Kandhi Hazara's house. She had been warned by the soldier who had admired her for so long that she must run away for the commander himself was coming to kill her. 'The gates will be opened for him,' she said.

But the commander had told his soldiers, 'As soon as the gates are opened, fire your weapons, do not hesitate, do not even use your eyes.' Kandhi Hazara waited in the moonlight, and ordered the gates to be opened when the commander called to her. When the gates were thrown open, the soldiers fired their weapons without a second's hesitation, and Kandhi Hazara was killed where she stood.

* * *

The feasting and dancing and music of the wedding went on until late and, with so much excitement, mischief came into my head. I said to my three friends, 'Soon all the women will sleep. Here is my plan. When the dancer sleeps, we'll creep up one at a time and kiss her. But only kiss her softly, on her cheek, so that she doesn't wake up. Put your hand into mine if you agree with this plan.' All of my friends put their hands into mine, because they didn't want to be cowards.

We waited until all the guests had left, and all the women guests had gone to a place where rugs and mattresses were set up for them to sleep. A bed had been provided for the dancer, because she was so honoured, and her bed was higher than any of the mattresses around her on which the other women slept. When we were sure that all the women were asleep, my first friend, Hussein, tiptoed between the sleeping women and reached the bed where the dancer slept. He kissed her on the cheek without waking her, then tiptoed back, picking his way so quietly and carefully that nobody awoke.

'What was it like?' we asked Hussein, and he spread his hands toward the sky and said, 'It is like kissing silk.'

My second friend, Yassim, took his turn, and he was just as careful as Hussein had been. He was successful, too, and couldn't wait to tell us how wonderful it was to kiss the dancer. 'It was better than anything I have ever done!' he said. 'It was like going to Heaven!'

I was about to send Hashim along next, but then an argument broke out. 'Why are you last?' my three friends asked me. 'Are you afraid? Surely you are!' But I explained that the last person to kiss the dancer would be in more danger than the first three, because after three kisses, she might stir and wake. So I chose the last kiss for myself. My friends could see that what I was saying was very intelligent, even though they didn't believe me, and my third friend Hashim went ahead of me. But Hashim was not so lucky as Hussein and Yassim, and his kiss woke the dancer. He came running back to our hiding place, stepping on sleeping women all the way so that by the time he reached us the night was full of screams and shouting. There would be very big trouble if we were caught. We ran like wild goats over fields and ditches and fences and hid ourselves safely until the morning. We knew that we could go home when it was light, and tell everyone that we became tired and fell asleep on the ground. Or if we had been recognised, then tempers would have cooled down by morning, maybe.

Well, there was trouble—of course there was trouble. But it was worth it. It was a great day for us, the day of Sayeed Assad's wedding. But if only Hashim hadn't woken the dancer, then it would have been perfect!

I thought to myself in the days after the wedding, 'Great things will come my way, surely. I am in the wide world now.'

7

School

WOOMERA IS A PRISON, certainly, but it is also a school. The coils of razor wire on top of vertical steel bars all around the perimeter, the high-security locks on the gates and the CCTV cameras mounted on walls and fences and poles, and in every room show you that the place is a serious prison, but you only understand why Woomera is also a school when you've been behind the wire for a few months.

In a school, you advance each year if you work hard and study hard and pay attention. In Woomera, you advance in the same way, but you don't have to wait a year; a few months is all it takes. The November intake camp, one of Woomera's four camps, is where your education starts, but just as a person feels puzzled and worried on his first day in school, so you feel puzzled and worried on your first day in November.

Approaching Woomera across the desert, all I could think

about was how sinister the place looked: many grey concrete buildings behind tall, glinting steel fences, the whole place standing completely by itself, no town in sight. One road led in; the same road led out. The desert air was so clear that the fences of Woomera stood out sharply against the blue sky and the sandy soil. When I say Woomera looked 'sinister', I don't mean sinister like a haunted castle, but like a place where dreadful scientific experiments might be carried out. Or where people might be put to death silently. It shocked us all in the bus, heading toward those gates. Australia was a modern country. Maybe this was what they built in modern countries—big, shining prisons where you could be left and forgotten. Not everyone would see it that way, but to a refugee like me, it looked inhuman. How much did I or any of the other asylum seekers on the bus with me really know about Australia? Maybe the stories we'd heard of people eventually finding safety were all lies. Maybe this was the end of everything.

Once in the camp, we started to relax just a little. There were no men in white coats rounding us up for experiments. The guards were friendly enough. But we still had to deal with our confusion. What was expected of us? Who was in charge, who were the bosses and big shots? How did you make a good impression? These things we learned little by little in the November section of Woomera. We learned that we were taking an examination, that the prison authorities were watching all the time, either on the spot or before a television monitor. Many of the tests we were being marked for, we were already well equipped to pass. Good manners, for example. The authorities liked good manners. We knew this because of their frowns and head-shaking whenever someone, usually out of frustration, said the wrong thing in the wrong tone of voice. The principal test in the canteen was the Don't-Jump-the-Queue test, the Wait-Your-Turn test; then there was the Don't-Be-Greedy test (by insisting on a bigger portion of rice, you could easily get very poor marks) and the What-Are-You, Some-Sort-of-Gourmet? test (you passed by not complaining about the same old dishes day after day).

The-Shut-Up-and-Eat test came next, and if you wanted to score well, you sat down at your table and got busy with your fork, instead of staring at the food as if you were listening to your wife nagging you. The Big-Smile test was an important one to pass, as we all came to understand. The authorities were judging whether you would be a pleasant person to have around in the land of Australia, and we all guessed that a big smile helped them to like you, and maybe want to keep you. Of course, you didn't want to go around with a big smile all day long, because then you would surely fail the Lunatic test.

All of these tests were easy to pass, really. Unless you were half mad with worry about your wife and children back in Afghanistan or Pakistan or Iran or Chechnya, or you were depressed and homesick, or you were full of anxiety about the possibility of being put into an aeroplane and taken back to the place you came from. Then they were hard to pass.

Most of the asylum seekers in Woomera recognised that they were being tested and did their best to impress the prison authorities. Certainly I knew that I was being watched and marked, but I must say that I never really went out of my way to score highly. If I smiled, it was because I felt like smiling. If I didn't make any complaints about the food, it was because the food was okay with me. Because even when you know you are

70

being tested, you can't make yourself into a whole new person just to impress the authorities. You can do that for a day or two, but after that it becomes almost impossible. The weight of worry in your brain won't let you smile sometimes. The feeling of having no power to make things happen gets into your heart and you begin to question whether you really are a human being like other human beings. You start to think, 'Have I lost something that used to be part of me? Has part of me become sick and died while the rest of my body is still living?'

※　※　※

A few weeks ago, I graduated from November to Mike—the second of the four camps that make up Woomera. Sierra and Main Camp are the other two. I hope to graduate again, from Mike to Main Camp. But I do not want to find out what Sierra is like. Sierra is for the bad people; those who beat up other inmates, or steal, or in some cases just make demands that the Woomera authorities don't want to hear. The ones who make demands of that sort are not bad people, but they get sent to Sierra anyway, a prison within a prison.

I have been made supervisor of the mess in Mike, and also leader of my Afghani group. The prison authorities believe that I am a helpful and co-operative person, and I think they also feel that the things I have told them about my life in Afghanistan and my reasons for coming here to Australia are probably true. They don't think that I am going to turn out to be a terrorist or a suicide bomber or a spy. I have scored high marks in the secret tests, I suppose. But now I have a problem. Every so often, a state policeman by the name of John comes to Mike to talk to us about Australian laws and Australian culture. He stands up before us in his uniform and always starts out by saying, 'Okay...' After the policeman says 'Okay...', I don't understand another word. I watch his lips moving and I watch him making gestures with his hands, but I have no idea what points he is trying to make. One time he seemed to be talking about illness, but it was hard to tell. He acted as if he were walking down a street with great difficulty, swaying and staggering. And so I thought, 'Is he saying that it is against the law to be sick in Australia? But that's crazy! How can a person help being sick?'

But then the policeman made some actions. He put his hand up to his mouth as if he was holding something, then he started to sway about and smile. Ah! I thought. He is drinking alcohol and now he is drunk! So I worked out that it must be against the law to be drunk in Australia. That's okay, I thought. Nothing good can come of being drunk. That is an easy law to obey. Other laws are a mystery to me. The English words come out of the policeman's mouth so rapidly and no matter how hard I try, I can't work out what laws he is talking about. Only one or two of the people listening have any idea of what is being said.

Afghanis in my group come to me after the policeman has been speaking and say, 'Najaf, what is all this about? You must tell us. You are the leader.' This is embarrassing for me. The Afghanis in my group rely on me. They trust me. I go for a walk around and about the place, trying to think of a solution. Probably I am being watched on the CCTV, and maybe I am also being tested. It might be the Problem-Solving Test, or maybe only the Tries-Hard Test. Whatever it is, I must work out something for the Afghanis, not because I want to pass any tests but because we all need to know what the policeman is saying. At least, I think we need to know. If I knew what the policeman was saying, I would know for sure if we need to know.

Then I remember a man who was on the boat with me, not an Afghani but an Iranian. And I remember that this man could speak some English, as well as his native Farsi, which is almost the same as Dari, the language of Afghanistan. How much, I'm not sure, because we didn't have much of an opportunity to speak English on a boat full of Afghanis and Iranians and Chechens. So I go off looking for this man, whose name is Shokr Ali. I find him with his friends, playing cards, and I ask him to come with me and listen to a proposal I have. We go outside and find a quiet place around the corner from the male ablution block.

'Shokr Ali, I am going to ask for your assistance.'

'In what way?'

'You speak English, I'm sure that's right.'

'Yes. You want me to teach you English?'

'No, not straight away. You know this policeman who comes and talks to us?'

'Yes, I know him. His name is John.'

'What does he talk about? I can't understand him.'

'Football. Cricket. Alcohol. Going out with women. Taxation. Driving a car.'

'Football?'

'Not football, truly. Not what we call football. Their own football. It's stupid, you don't want to know anything about it. And cricket. Hoo! Madness.'

'My friend,' I say, 'we both honour the same God. In His name, I implore you, interpret for my Afghanis. We must learn about things. About taxation, and driving a car. Not so much going out with women. Okay, maybe a little about that. Not for me, I am married, thank God, but for the single men.'

Shokr Ali is a good man. He wants to help me. I wait for his decision, and when it comes, it is what I want to hear. He says he will interpret for my Afghanis.

No sooner do I arrange for Shokr Ali to help us next time the policeman comes than I begin to worry about the food. I don't mean the type of food, but about everyone getting equal shares. This is a big problem. People here are very tense. If you remain tense and worried for long enough, you can begin to go mad. Just imagine this situation: You've been in Woomera for three months. You haven't had one hour in all that time, even in your sleep, when you have stopped worrying. You don't know what the Australians intend to do with you. You feel like screaming at the top of your voice. When you go to the mess for your lunch, you see that the person in front of you seems to have a very full plate but when it is your turn, your plate is only half full. You think, 'They are trying to starve me to death!' This is crazy, but because you are crazy, it seems completely true. If the person in front of you is a Pakistani and you are an Afghani, the next thing you think might be, 'They are trying to starve all the Afghanis to death!' Then you scream out loud, 'The Pakistanis are their favourites! They are starving the Afghanis!' And maybe you try to grab the plate of the Pakistani, except instead of giving you his plate, he punches you on the nose. The security officers come running to break up the fight, and they succeed, but alas!—you have failed the Peaceful-Fellow test. A big black mark will go on your file. Because when you have nothing to do and you feel as if you have no power and the days drag on and on, food becomes much more important than normal. Maybe you are getting more food in Woomera than you ever did back where you came from, but all that you can think of is that someone else is getting more. And because you are thinking so much these days about justice and injustice, standing up for your right to have a very full plate makes you lose all sight of the bigger picture.

I hate to imagine that my Afghanis could end up being sent back to Kabul because of a spoonful of rice and half a potato. I think of the men in my group struggling to stay alive when they were being hunted by the Taliban, then paying every bit of money they could raise to pay a people smuggler. I think of them hiding in the back of a van with a blanket over them while guards outside are paid off to allow the van to cross one frontier, and then another frontier. I think of them on a boat with water getting deeper and deeper in the hold each day and no pumps to discharge it. I think of these men finally setting foot on the land of Australia after all they have survived, and in the end being sent back to the Taliban because they've gone crazy over something that probably cost about 20 cents in Australian money. No, I couldn't bear it.

It seems to me that the solution must be to have somebody in the kitchen that the Afghanis trust when it is the turn of my countrymen to be fed. If they are having their plates filled by a Pakistani or an Iranian, they always think that they are being given too little. So I put an Afghani in charge of filling the plates when Afghanis are being served, and I tell him to make sure that every single person gets the same amount of food. When the Afghanis have finished eating, I call out to them, 'If you are still hungry, come for more!' In this way, we have peace.

Three weeks pass without any further trouble in the mess. One day in Mike camp, I stand at the counter in the mess from where the food is served, waiting to call up those who are still hungry. I myself haven't eaten yet, and the smell of the food is making me long for the half hour to pass so that I can sit down at a table and eat. But even though I'm hungry, I am happy. I look at the Afghanis eating and I think, 'What a beautiful thing peace is!' For I like peace. It is part of me, something that was inside of my brain and my heart when my mother gave birth to me. As I stand quietly watching, with the security guards at the door not even bothering to pay us much attention because we no longer have a reputation for arguing, I feel my lips making a smile. It is not the sort of smile that you make when you have heard a joke or because you wish to be friendly or because you think the CCTV cameras are watching and you want to score well in the Friendly-Fellow test. It is the smile that spreads on your face when you begin to hope, and when you think that the hope is not foolish. I enjoyed feeling hope for myself in my own situation, yes, but much more than that, I enjoyed being able to hope for everyone in the mess, all those eating their rice and stew and potatoes.

And what test was I taking in the School of Mike? The test that showed I could still feel happy.

8

The King's Son and the Canary Birds

ONCE MY FAMILY HAD moved to Mazar-e-Sharif, Gorg Ali began to look at me a little differently from the way he had in Shar Shar. I was considered just a child when we lived in the village. Minding the sheep was a suitable job for a child, or for a boy, at least. As long as I showed myself to be a reliable keeper of sheep, not much else was expected of me. But in the big city, there were no sheep for me to mind and Gorg Ali had to consider what sort of trade I might follow.

He was a kind and gentle man, Gorg Ali, as I have said. When he was looking at me in this new and mystifying way, he was actually trying to judge the sort of work I might handle well. He wanted me to be satisfied in my work. There are very few holidays for most Afghani workers; no long weekends, no sick days, no annual leave. An Afghani toils for most of his life on not much pay, so it is best if he likes what he is doing. This is not

77

to say that there is a lot of choice for a boy like me without a proper education, but Gorg Ali probably hoped that I would get some pleasure out of my trade, whatever that trade was to be.

During this time when a trade was being sought for me, Gorg Ali told me a story to prepare me for this new stage of my life. We had been building the roof of the new house but had stopped for rest and to eat some lunch. Gorg Ali called to me to sit beside him and offered me the water bottle.

He said, 'Soon all the work will be done, and our home will be here in Mazar-e-Sharif. And what then?'

I knew that there was a right answer and a wrong answer to my brother's question, but I didn't know what the right answer would be. So I said, 'What then? Ah, yes, that's a good question.'

Gorg Ali said, 'Have you heard the tale of the king's son?'

'No, I haven't heard any tales about the king's son.' I was becoming a little anxious about this whole conversation. In my experience, when an older person decides to tell you a story, it is to soften you up for something unpleasant.

'Well,' said Gorg Ali, 'it seems there was a prince who had reached an age when the question of marriage becomes important. Do you know what I mean?'

I said, 'Yes, of course,' but really I had no idea.

'Now, the king's son—the prince, that is—had lived an easy life, as the sons of kings always do. He did not have to go into the fields and turn the soil for crops. He did not have to gather firewood for the oven. He did not have to pick fruit from the trees to sell in the market. He did not have to keep an eye on the sheep and chase away the wolves. No, the king had servants to do all that sort of work. And so the king's son stayed in his bed until late in the morning, and when he roused himself, a servant placed his breakfast before him and wrapped a warm robe on his shoulders and poured tea for him. And when breakfast was finished, the king's son went to the library and read books, or he walked in the garden and listened to the birds singing.'

I thought to myself, 'Lucky him!'

'But it happened one day,' said Gorg Ali, 'that the king's son wandered from his great house where he lived with his father and his mother and his brothers and his 500 servants down into the village, and there he chanced to see a poor village girl whose beauty was so great that canary birds flew down from the trees and sat by her as she swept the threshold of her father's house. The king's son thought to himself, "Who would make me happier than this girl? I will ask my father to talk to her father and mother, and so arrange a marriage." '

Gorg Ali looked into the embers of the small fire we kept going in the cold weather as he told this story, but every now and again he would turn his head and look me in the face, perhaps to make sure that I was paying attention. And I was paying attention. I wanted to hear what befell the king's son, for it was obvious to me that this story must have a twist in it somewhere.

'So the king's son spoke to his father. "Sir," he said, "I have been to the village and there I saw the girl I wish to marry. She is only a poor girl, but so beautiful that the canary birds fly down from the trees and sit by her as she sweeps the threshold of her father's house."

The king said to his son, "God willing, she will be your wife and bear your children." The king sent his wife to talk with the mother of the girl, while the king himself spoke with the girl's father. Naturally, the girl's parents felt honoured that their daughter had attracted the admiration of the king's son.

But alas, when they told their daughter of the king's son's love, she said, "No, I will not marry the king's son."

The father and mother went in great distress to the king and said, "Our daughter has set her mind against your son, although as for her heart, we cannot say."

And the king said, "You amaze me! Has your daughter given a cause?"

"No," said the father. "She will only tell the cause to your son himself."

So the king's son went with his broken heart to the beautiful girl and asked her, "What cause can there be that you spurn me in this way? I would sit you in a great house and give you servants to take the burden from your shoulders."

The girl said to the king's son, "Sir, today you are the king's son, but tomorrow, who can say? How would you keep me and provide for our children? Can you grow grain in the fields? Can you catch fish in the stream? Find a skill to turn your hand to if times turn bad, and then ask me again."

The king's son laughed to hear this, but he went to a man who made grass matting and asked to be taught the craft, and so in time he became a master. Then the girl he had set his heart on accepted him gladly and they were married and raised six children. But alas, a time came when the king's throne was taken from him after a battle with another king, and the king and his family and his son and beautiful daughter-in-law were exiled. It fell to the king's son to keep the wolf from the door, and how did he manage that?'

'By making grass matting?' I answered.

'So it was,' said Gorg Ali, and we sat quietly looking at the fire while the lesson of the story sank into my brain.

'This means,' I said, after thinking for a few minutes, 'that I must find a skill?'

'That's it,' said Gorg Ali.

'Will I make grass matting?'

'No,' said Gorg Ali.

'Then what?'

'There's a man I know. He will train you.'

'Train me to do what, though?'

'You will see,' said Gorg Ali.

I spent a few days wondering what skill I would be told to learn. I was glad it wasn't to be making grass matting, because that would be boring. Grass matting can only be made in two or three ways, and after a year of it, I would probably be ready to cut my own throat. I didn't like the idea of making mud bricks for my whole life, either. I didn't like the idea of making anything that barely changed from day to day. I liked to work with things that made you think; things that gave some work to your brain as well as to your hands. But as it turned out, my older brothers set me to work in a place where there was very little work for my brain: they sent me to a blacksmith's shop.

Now, I am very sure that a master blacksmith has a lot of work to occupy his brain, and I'm sure he can find great satisfaction in his craft. The blacksmith I was sent to work with, Hallim, was not a man such as that. He was not a blacksmith of the old sort, who might be asked to make one thing one day and another thing the next, and a third thing the day after that. He was never asked to make a bridle for a horse or a magnificent sword for a warrior or special iron shoes for the warrior's horse. His shop had more to do with welding than with anything else, and welding is not much fun, unless you happen to be a bit crazy. As soon as I walked into Hallim's shop, I knew I would hate the job I was supposed to give my whole life to. It was a dirty, noisy shop where five welders and smiths laboured furiously from six-thirty in the morning until six-thirty at night. No sooner had I stepped onto the floor of the workshop than my face was covered with a gritty mixture of metal filings and dust. Men walked around with lengths of steel that they threw with a great crash to the floor. Other men in welding masks touched the tips of metal welding rods to sheets of steel, producing a sound like very loud radio static and storms of bright sparks. And then there was the hammering, which went on all day as steel was twisted and wrought into shape. The shop was like something you would expect to find in Hell, if you were unlucky enough to end up there.

Hallim, who was a good man and very strong, took me around the shop and showed me what was being made. Fashioning iron bed-frames took up a great deal of his time, followed by making the casing for air-conditioning units of the sort we use in Afghanistan—no refrigeration, just a fan between sheets of insulation, and a water tank. This all looked very uninspiring to me, but I tried not to show how unhappy I was at the prospect of working in Hallim's shop for the rest of my life. I thought, 'Najaf, you are not a king's son and you cannot look for a job just to please a pretty girl. You must work.' So I settled into my new occupation, and tried to ignore the noise and the grit and the monotony.

I was not good at welding, which was my main task each day. I did not prepare the surfaces that were to be joined in the proper way, and so my welds failed to hold. It was not that I deliberately neglected the instructions of the other welders who were training me. No, I listened as carefully as I could, but at a certain point my mind switched itself off, as if something in me had decided all by itself that welding would not be important in my life and was saving space in my memory for other things—although what would those other things be? I simply didn't like metal. Some people I knew—Abdul Ali, for one—loved working with metal, loved its qualities. But to me, it was a lifeless material. It had no voice. It didn't speak to me. As I struggled with it, I would hiss, 'Stupid stuff, you are! Stupid, stupid, stupid!' After hours of cursing the metal and hours of making a mess of the welds, I would stop and stare out the door and whisper, 'Najaf, what are you doing here? Are you mad? This isn't for you. Run away! Run away!'

I didn't run away. I stuck with the tasks that were set for me in Hallim's shop, but from early morning until sundown, a smile was never to be seen on my face. When I reached home at the end of the day, I complained to my mother about the work. The welding flashes had burst small blood vessels in my eyes, leaving them bloodshot and aching. As an apprentice, I was expected to make do without a welding helmet. When your eyes ache, it is like a toothache. You can't ignore it and the constant pain makes you miserable. My mother did what she could for me, cutting slices from potatoes and laying them on my eyes when I went to bed. The juices of the potato helped to reduce the swelling. But the next day, the welding flashes would undo all of the good work of the potato juices.

I complained to my brothers, too, but they paid no attention. Even Gorg Ali simply shrugged. Afghani men don't complain about physical hardship, and they don't complain about pain. Boys are allowed to complain a little, but only while they are getting used to what they will have to endure all their lives. So when Gorg Ali and Abdul Ali shrugged and said, 'Just get on with it, Najaf,' what they meant was for me to face up to life and accept aching eyes as a price I had to pay.

Gorg Ali said to me one day, 'I work hard too. Do you hear me crying about it?' Probably he was disappointed that my job didn't satisfy me, since he wanted me to be happy in my occupation, but that didn't mean he was going to search around for something else for me to do. He had taken over from my father, and it was his responsibility to see that I became a man. He couldn't afford to listen to me grizzling. Abdul Ali was the same. 'Where would I be if I troubled the ears of those around me with my problems?' he said.

It didn't seem to me that Gorg Ali and Abdul Ali had as much to complain about in their trades as I did. Gorg Ali was a tinsmith and a beekeeper. The work of a tinsmith was not like that of a welder; not so dirty and noisy. Gorg Ali made metal trunks and suitcases; there was real craft in his trade. And the beehives in the fields of Shar Shar that he returned to each week gave him a break from the hammer and the tinsnips and the soldering iron, took him into the hills and the fresh air. Abdul Ali was a butcher. He kept cattle and slaughtered them himself, in the traditional way. He hung the fresh meat from the branches of our berry bushes along the front of our property, the bright colour of the bloody flesh surrounded by the bright red of the berries. People came and chose their meat while it was still hanging. I had no desire to spend my life cutting the throats of cattle and catching the blood in a tub, but it would have been better than welding. Even digging big holes in the ground and filling them in again would have been better than welding.

Very little was asked of my younger brother Rosal Ali, partly because he was too young to work and partly because he was hopelessly irresponsible. Life for him, even as a child, was a playground, and the sort of play that delighted him most was mischief. He always looked for a chance to turn some simple task he was given into a catastrophe. Just as my older brothers were forever lecturing me about my responsibilities, so I lectured Rosal Ali about his.

'Is a demon living inside your skin? Learn to do what you are told!'

But Rosal Ali would shrug and smile and go on his way, happy to have made me angry, as if that was his great project in life. And the harder I worked as a welder and the more I hated it, the angrier Rosal Ali made me.

Maybe my anger with Rosal Ali was to do with the freedom he gave himself when my own freedom was fading away to nothing. I walked to work in the early morning with a great weight resting on my heart, and when I turned the last corner and saw Hallim raising the steel roller door of the welding shop with a crash, the weight grew heavier still. I asked myself why I was so unhappy and answered myself with all the complaints I have already mentioned—the noise and the dirt and the pain. But another reason, probably the most important one of all, was that I knew I would never be a good welder; I would never feel any joy in what I did; I would never make something beautiful and wish to praise God for the skill he had put in my hands. Somewhere in my heart was the knowledge that the welding shop was not where I was meant to be; it was not my destiny.

In my head and heart and in my soul too, I knew that God intended me for a different fate, and so I could only think that God was busy somewhere else and had not noticed that He had left me suffering in Hallim's welding shop. I was like one of the canary birds that Hallim kept in cages in his shop—for Hallim loved these little birds, and delighted in hearing their song. The little yellow birds had no place in a welding shop; they should have been out in the open air, flashing across the blue sky. God had not intended them to live in cages while all around men hammered iron and steel. The songs they sang in their cages were not songs of joy, as Hallim believed, but songs of despair.

On my way to the welding shop each morning and on my way home each evening I passed the Rawze-e-Sharif, or in English, the Blue Mosque that houses the Shrine of Hazrat Ali, the fourth caliph of Islam. The mosque is one of the most beautiful in all Islam with ceramic tiles of blue and gold cladding the outside. Each time I passed the mosque I offered a prayer to Allah that I should be rescued from the toil and pain of the welding shop. It took months before it came to me that God was unlikely to pick me up by the shoulders and carry me to a place where I could work at a more satisfying job. The task of God was only to remind me of how much I hated what I was doing, and He carried out that task with great dedication. Changing things for the better was up to me. I had strong arms, a good brain, and these were God's gifts to me to use. Waiting for a miracle would get me nowhere. And so when I made this discovery, I gave my thanks to Allah and to Hazrat Ali and began to think in a different way.

'Najaf,' I said, 'God helps him who helps himself. Are you locked in a cage? No! You have feet to carry you about, you have eyes to see. Let your feet carry you to a happier occupation, and let your eyes guide you along the way.'

And so it was.

* * *

Like most other people, I hope for good fortune in my life and try to avoid bad fortune. I touch wood to help good fortune find its way into my life; I throw salt over my shoulder if I spill any; I don't open umbrellas inside, because for some strange reason, opening an umbrella indoors brings catastrophes down on people's heads. Or so it is said. I am as superstitious as the next person, as you can see. But why are we superstitious? Why do people all over the world invent hundreds of ways, thousands of ways of helping good luck along and hindering bad luck? It must be because we don't know where good fortune comes from, or where bad fortune comes from, and so we are forced to guess. But there is one thing I know about good fortune: if it comes up to you and shakes your hand, you must greet it like a friend, sit down with it over a glass of tea, smile at it just as it smiles at you.

One day, making my way home from the welding shop, I met a boy a few years older than me who had once been our neighbour in Shar Shar. Sarwah was his name.

'Is it Najaf, from my village? My greetings to your family. But tell me, Najaf, why is your face so long? You look as if you have a pain in your stomach.'

'No, Sarwah,' I said. 'No pain in my stomach. I am well, except for my eyes.'

And I explained to Sarwah that my work in the welding

shop made my eyes ache. Sarwah didn't say anything for a few minutes, but he listened to my complaints about my occupation as we walked along past the shops that were closing for the day.

'I have a job that pleases me,' he said. 'It's good to work when your job gives you pleasure.'

'I am sure of that,' I said. 'But what is your job, Sarwah?'

'I am a rugmaker in the factory of Najaf, your namesake.'

'Is that so?' I said, and I felt immediately that Sarwah had enjoyed better fortune than me in his occupation. A rugmaker!

'Maybe you should find another job,' said Sarwah.

'Yes, another job would be good, I agree.'

'Maybe you should find a job that doesn't hurt your eyes,' said Sarwah.

'A job that doesn't hurt my eyes would be good, I agree.'

'You could work for Najaf, as I do. You could learn to make rugs.'

'Learn to make rugs?'

'Do you think that would be better for your eyes? Surely it would.'

'Certainly! But how can I tell my brothers? They think that working in a welding shop is a very good job.'

'Well, that's your task, I can't do that for you. You tell your brothers, then come and work for Najaf.'

'When?'

'As soon as you like,' said Sarwah.

'Now?'

'No, not now,' said Sarwah. 'Now it is dark. Come tomorrow. I will show you where Najaf's factory is found.'

I didn't say anything to Abdul Ali when I reached home. I didn't say anything to Gorg Ali. I didn't say anything to

my mother. But my heart was so full that they could see that
something was going on.

'A good day, was it?' said Abdul Ali.

'A very good day,' I said.

'You like your work better now?'

'Oh yes,' I said. 'Much better.'

'Do you see, it is as I said. If you persist, you enjoy your work.
I am proud of you.'

The next day, I didn't go anywhere near the welding shop.
I didn't want to face Hallim and tell him that I was leaving.
Instead I found Najaf's factory and asked for Sarwah, who took
me to Najaf and said many kind things about me to his boss.

Najaf looked at me sceptically and tugged at the lobe of his
ear while Sarwah was singing my praises. He shrugged when
the introduction was over and said, 'Okay, if he's as good as
you say we'll give him a try. See what the others think of him.'

Sarwah took me to one of the rooms of the factory and
introduced me to the men and boys working at the looms.

'This is Najaf, from my village of Shar Shar. He has come to
learn the craft. I know his family well, and it is an honourable
family. His father was esteemed in Shar Shar, and his brothers
are esteemed in his place, now that his father has departed
for Heaven.'

Sarwah's teachers listened to him without saying that they
would accept me or reject me. They looked me over in a friendly
way, then nodded their heads to show that I would be given a
chance. I said a silent prayer of thanks and resolved to prove
that Sarwah's kind words were truthful. After all, how many
opportunities does God provide? One or two, sometimes a third,
but He doesn't humour us forever. God had placed Sarwah in

my path, and for that I was grateful. It was now my task to show thanks with hard work.

I worked hard from the first hour of that first day in the weaving trade. I could see that one day, the trade might become special to me. I was still a boy, still only 12 years old, and my tasks that day and for months to come were simple ones—monotonous ones, to tell the truth.

But let me begin by describing how a weaving factory is set up in Afghanistan. First, what I call a 'factory' is not what people in Western countries would call a factory, for the looms are usually erected in the house of the owner. Of course the factory owner must have a big enough house to start with, and Najaf's house was indeed big. He had set three rooms aside for the weaving, and in each room three looms were kept working. Two students worked at each loom, supervised by a teacher. One student worked on the borders of the rug, while the second student worked on the design. In each room, an apprentice as young as me would sit on the floor winding wool around an oblong of smooth wood in an intricate way, so that the wool grew into a large ball, the size and shape of a big watermelon, and from these balls the weavers would draw the yarn. Looking into a room you would see ten people at work: mentors, students and an apprentice. As the weavers work they bend back and forward, tying the knots along the warp of the rug, drawing the yarn straight with an iron comb and passing the shuttle between the taut strands of the yarn to form the weft. You would also see the teachers watching closely and making corrections and giving advice. And you would see the apprentice busily winding the wool. Everybody works hard, with great concentration, but at the same time the weavers and teachers and even the apprentice chatter and joke and sing. Fragments of yarn float in the air and settle on the floor.

This was the life I was about to begin—the life of the rugmaker. With one glance around the room, I could take in all the stages of the career that awaited me—apprentice, student, teacher. It was a life that I welcomed.

Two weeks after I started work at the factory of Najaf, I still hadn't said anything about my change of career to my brothers or to my mother. I arrived home each night looking much more cheerful and without the grit of the welding shop under my nails, but my brothers thought that was just because I was enjoying my work now and maybe washing my hands more carefully. My eyes were no longer red and aching, but they probably thought that I was getting used to the work and no longer suffering a reaction to the welding flashes. I was not paid a wage either as a welder or a rugmaker (apprentices are not paid in Afghanistan) but each Friday night at the welding shop I'd been given a few coins to buy sweets with, just as I was at Najaf's factory. Instead of buying sweets, I saved the coins in a wooden moneybox. My family could see that I was still saving coins, so no suspicions were aroused. Then one evening when I arrived home from work, my brother Abdul Ali asked me to sit beside him at the evening meal.

Now, Abdul Ali didn't have the gentle manner of Gorg Ali (who was away somewhere that evening) and it was unusual for him to show me affection in this way. But I accepted his invitation to sit beside him at dinner without any foreboding and enjoyed the novelty of his arm around my shoulder.

'So how are things going at the welding shop?' he asked me. 'You seem happier these days. I'm glad to see that.'

'Oh, yes, much happier,' I said. 'Everything is fine at the shop. No problems at all.'

'It does my heart good to hear that, little one. And you're getting along with all the people you work with? No arguments?'

'No arguments, brother. I like the people I work with.'

'And you're learning more and more each day, I suppose?'

'Yes, brother, I learn all the time.'

'So we can expect that you will be a master in your own right before long?'

'God willing!' I said.

'Only, it's a funny thing,' said Abdul Ali, with his arm gripping me more and more firmly around the shoulders, 'but I was out that way today—out near Hallim's welding shop. And I thought to myself, "I'll just stop by and say hello to my little brother, and congratulate him on settling down to his tasks as he has." That's what I thought. And so do you know what I did?'

My heart sank to the pit of my stomach, although I tried to keep smiling.

'No,' I said. 'What did you do, brother?'

'I called into the shop. That's what I did. And I said to my old friend Hallim, "Blessings on you and your family, Hallim! I've come to greet my little brother, Najaf. I've come to congratulate him on settling down to his tasks. But where is he, Hallim? I don't see him. Has he stepped out to the toilet? Or have you sent him to the shop for tea? Tell me where he is, because I want to put my arm around his shoulders and hug him tight!"'

I tried to squirm out of Abdul Ali's grip, but he was holding me too firmly.

'And do you know what Hallim said to me, little brother? Do you know what he said?'

I didn't answer. How could I?

'He said these words to me. "Oh, Najaf disappeared two weeks ago. We haven't seen so much as his shadow since then." That's what Hallim said to me.'

And with that, Abdul Ali gave me a mighty blow across the side of my head, such that I saw stars spinning in front of my eyes.

'What do you mean lying to us in this way?' he shouted at me. 'What do you mean? You're a disgrace to your father's family!' And he gave me another great whack with the flat of his hand.

'Oh, son, beware of your strength!' my mother said to Abdul Ali. 'Don't harm the boy!'

I was by this time howling my eyes out, and at the same time trying to blubber out my explanation. 'I'm making rugs! I'm making rugs! I met Sarwah in the street!'

'You met who? You're doing what?' said Abdul Ali.

'Let him talk, son,' said my mother. 'God gives us all a chance to repent.'

And so I was permitted to sit upright once more and explain myself. I told Abdul Ali all about meeting Sarwah and going to Najaf's factory and sitting on the floor to wind the wool onto the spools. I told him that I would one day become a student working at the loom, and that eventually I would become a master myself. I told him that I loved the work I did, and that Najaf the owner of the factory was pleased with me, and that the students were pleased with me, and the teachers were pleased with me.

Abdul Ali was watching me closely with his hand in his beard.

By the time I'd finished my tale, tears were running down my face. In the way that children are able to judge the moods of their masters in a crisis, I could see that my explanation had calmed my brother down considerably. A slightly more generous light had come into his eyes.

'This story will be tested,' he said to me. 'I will speak to this Najaf who has a rug factory, as you say.'

'Speak to him, brother, with all my heart,' I said. 'I like this work. I will turn my hand to rug-making all my life. I am not lazy.'

'No,' said Abdul Ali, 'I will grant that you are not lazy. Eat your food.'

Peace was restored. And yet, I resented deeply those two blows to my head. Was it not possible for my brother to simply ask me for an explanation without boxing my ears? Truly, that was something like the way of the Taliban—first, punish, don't bother about explanations. At the same time, I had to admit that I should have told my family when I moved from welding to rug-making.

Maybe the boxing of my ears was the punishment of God Himself. 'You complained of the job I found for you in the welding shop,' He must have been saying to me, 'so I found you a job better suited to your nature. But you were not honest. Accept this boxing of your ears for telling white lies, and go about your work. Fair's fair, Najaf.'

9

Main Camp

I HAVE AT LAST GRADUATED to Main Camp, and although it's only a shift of 200 metres from Mike, it makes me feel that something good has happened; that progress has been made. Moving me anywhere would have produced the same feeling, no doubt. When I was told I would be moving, I thought, 'Ah, Najaf, you have worked hard and shown how reliable you are, and they like you, so this is your reward.' But it was foolish of me to think in that way. Even if the Canberra Australians intend to send me back to Mazar-e-Sharif to be shot, they would first send me to Main Camp. And the truth is that Main Camp is a very tense place. From here, there are only two places you can go: into the land of Australia, or to the country that you came here from.

When people first arrive at Woomera, they know that they will be in the camp for a few months, at least; maybe for many months. They know that there are many questions to be asked before a decision about their future is made. They know, after a few weeks, that they will be moved to Mike and then to Main Camp, even if the Australians don't intend to give them a visa. And even though they are worried, they know at least that this gamble they have taken is not going to come to an end overnight. But here in Main Camp, it is as if we are all waiting for a knock on the door, and that knock will mean either great happiness, or the worst unhappiness in the world.

First in November, then in Mike, and now in Main Camp, I have been building up a picture of the land outside of Woomera. I caught glimpses of towns and cities from the bus on the way here. I have spoken to about 50 Australians. I have seen pictures of Australia. I have heard the policeman talking about culture and law and sport and politics. And I am sure, very sure, that I want to stay here.

I can see in my mind's eye Najaf walking down the streets of the big cities and stopping to look in the windows of shops. I can see Najaf the immigrant stopping once more in his walk to think about the shop that he might have one day. In the window he would place a big, beautiful Baluchi rug with fine borders and a pattern that would make people stop and say, 'My God, such a rug!'

Inside the shop I would have a thousand more rugs. The people who have stopped to stare at the Baluchi come into my shop—I see them walking through the doorway. But I do not run up to them and throw my arms around them and say, 'Thank you, thank you for coming into my shop!' No, I stay seated at my work table, but I smile at the visitors. 'You are welcome,' I say. 'Look around. Take your time.' In the bazaar of Mazar-e-Sharif, people with rugs to sell call out to the tourists, 'Please, very beautiful rugs here, please you come, most beautiful rugs in Afghanistan!' But I will not do that. My shop will be a place where people can relax. If they want to know about the rugs, I will tell them. If they want to buy, I will sell. But I won't be pushy.

I know this word 'pushy' now; it is the same as 'shalla', as we say in Dari. Somebody who is 'shalla' grabs hold of you and won't let go. He keeps hold of you all the way down the street, like a dog who has taken your trousers in his teeth. Finally you must say to this shalla person, 'In the name of God, let me enjoy my peace!' I can see that Australians don't like people to be pushy, and I don't like it either, so we will suit each other, surely.

What else do I know of this country I have come to after such a long journey? Cars—many cars here. Everyone has a car, it is said. Some people have two cars. Even women have cars. Most of the cars I saw from the bus on the way here were new. And the people drove carefully. How wonderful it would be to have a new car—a car that I could wash every day so that it stayed bright in the sunshine! And I would sweep the inside so that it was always clean, and I would have perhaps a small picture of the Prophet on the ledge at the front of the car near the steering wheel, and a picture of Hakima and a picture of Maria, so that I could see them every moment while I drive. First, of course, I must learn how to drive. In Afghanistan, this is no big problem. You get a car, you drive the car.

So, Najaf the immigrant has a shop with a beautiful Baluchi rug in the window, and a car with a picture of the Prophet on the ledge at the front and a picture of Hakima and a picture of Maria. Then it is most important that I have a house to live in—a house to bring my wife and daughter to. The house must have a good kitchen and a toilet inside, as the custom is in Australia, and a shower and rugs on the floor and a woven wall hanging, and pots to go in the cupboards and beautiful plates and bowls, and a stove for cooking. Maybe at first I will have a small house, an apartment, a place of comfort but inexpensive. But if I have good fortune and the people who come to my shop buy my rugs and tell their friends to come and buy my rugs, it is possible that I will have a house with a garden one day. Such a joy that would be! Flowers would grow there in the garden, and who knows—maybe watermelons?

* * *

Daydreams do me no harm, so long as I remember that I am still in Main Camp. Some people have daydreams, then they believe that they are entitled to what they dreamed about. This is foolishness. My daydreams are only for my amusement; I don't share them with other people. I know that I could be sent back to Afghanistan. I haven't forgotten that. If that happens, so be it. It will make me unhappy, but God expects that we can survive such disappointments. He has given us sufficient strength.

I am not tense, like so many of the people here. I have told the Australians only the truth. I cannot live if I am making myself sick with worry. So let it remain in the hands of the Australians. And I must be strong in my body and my mind for whatever happens. Even if the Australians keep me, there will be so much hard work to make a new life here. I think of this need to remain strong as I clean up in the Main Camp mess. I think of a story I was told as a boy; the story of an old camel, a strong beast who lived in the north of Afghanistan. He was owned by a master who made the beast carry great loads on his back. He would be burdened with bags of wheat, or house bricks, or even huge sacks of watermelons. As it happened, the old camel had a son, a fine young creature who was not yet used to a life of bearing great loads. The young camel would lament long and loud when a load was placed on his back, and in his own language would curse the master who had so burdened him. One day, the old camel, the father of the young camel, called to him: 'Listen to me, I have good advice for you!' And the young camel stopped complaining for a minute to hear what his father had to say. The old camel said, 'We are both burdened with heavy loads, isn't that true?' And the young camel said, 'True enough, father, and a great injustice it is!' The old camel said, 'Son, lift your head and tell me what you see.' The young camel said, 'I see the sky and the mountains.' The old camel said, 'Now look down at your feet. What do you see?' And the young camel said, 'I see the path on which my feet stand.' The old camel said, 'Where does that path lead, tell me that?' The young camel said, 'The path leads onward and onward to the mountains and beyond the mountains.' The old camel said, 'Come what may, we must climb those mountains. If you lament now, what will be left when the real work begins?'

Main Camp is a place of tension, as I said. And it is a place of tears. Many people had kept their hopes alive through months in November, months in Mike, only to have their dreams wither in Main Camp when the message arrived from the Australians of Canberra: 'Visa denied.' These people who had been rejected were both sorrowful and confused. They had seen others leaping into the air with happiness when news of acceptance arrived. A person who had not been successful with the Australians would ask himself, 'Why not me? My case was as good as any. Why have some from my city been accepted by the Australians, while I am cast aside?' Hope is like a little child who must be cared for and clothed and fed each day, and when hope is destroyed, it is as if the child has died, despite all of the care and love. It is not just disappointment I see when people receive bad news; it is grief.

One case of rejection makes my heart ache more than any other, for I know the justice of this man's claim; I know his story is true. But the Australians say that he is telling lies and is not an Afghani as he says. How Australians recognise each other in a foreign land, I do not know. Perhaps they don't. Perhaps they must wait until they hear a person's accent before they can be sure that the person is Australian. But it is different for Afghanis. I know if a person is from my homeland without listening to him talk. I know if he is Afghani by the way he walks, by the way he stands. Even more than these signs, I know another Afghani by his eyes and the way he looks back at me. When he sees me, his eyes say, 'Yes, you are right, we have seen the same sights in our lives, we have seen the same sky and moon, we have seen the seasons change, we have seen the red flowers in spring.' If you are not Afghani, you cannot make me believe that you are. There is no trick you can play that will make me believe you. And so when the Australians said to this man, 'You are not Afghani, you have told us lies', I knew that a terrible mistake had been made. It is not possible for refugees like me to give evidence to the Australians about another refugee. They will not listen.

They say, 'Oh ho, you have made a pact with this man!'

I want to say to the Australians, 'On my life, this man is Afghani, you have made a big error here!' Instead, I share his sorrow and tears come to my eyes just as they come to his. 'Brother, we know you spoke the truth,' I say to this poor man. 'Surely the Australians will discover their mistake.' He raises his hands and lets them fall, then continues on his way with his head bowed low.

Half an hour later, I am walking around the compound, shaking my head. Nobody likes to see injustice. It gets into your heart and fills you with pain. In the midst of my thoughts, I hear my name called. I look up to see a lady I know well hurrying towards me. When she reaches me, she raises her hands to the sky and laments loudly.

'What is it, sister? What has happened?'

She tells me that the man I had spoken to a short time before has sewn his lips together. 'A horror!' she says. 'God comfort him!'

I run to the dormitory in which this man lives. It is in E Block, some distance from my own dormitory in B Block. From my side of the wire fence that closes off the E Block dormitory, I see the poor, wretched man squatting outside the door with his head bowed and his hands dangling loosely beside him. Blood is gushing from his mouth and down the front of his shirt.

I cry out, 'Help him! Bring help!' I am sick to my stomach; I have never been able to look at flowing blood without feeling ill in this way.

Security guards—perhaps eight or ten of them—arrive and try to seize the man and take him away. But his friends won't let the guards take him, and soon people are wrestling and struggling and shouting loudly. Some of the poor man's friends are dashing their heads against the wall of the dormitory, injuring themselves in solidarity. Many of these people have also been refused visas and are waiting in despair for deportation. About 40 such people, nearly all of them Afghanis, are part of this terrible struggle. I am doubled up with a hand over my mouth to prevent myself vomiting. The whole scene of struggle with the unhappy man in the centre, with his blood running in streams from his mouth, is like a picture from Hell. I am feeling powerless and miserable. Although there is a gate through the fence to E Block dormitory, I can't enter. These people don't know me and will likely strike out at me in their frenzy. I can do nothing. This man's heart has been torn into pieces, but because everyone has seen broken hearts before and there's nothing unique about such pain, he has had to mutilate himself to show us all what it feels like.

It is as if he has said, 'Can you not see now what sorrow your disbelief has caused? You have called me a liar, but this mouth told you only the truth.'

Finally the guards subdue the man and his friends and take him away to be treated. And I? I shuffle back to my own dormitory, saddened to the depths of my soul. What I am thinking is this: Australians, would it have been such a tragedy if you had accepted this man's story? Would your country have been destroyed if you had shown a little more kindness? Surely not.

* * *

A week has passed since the protest in E Block, and now we have a new protest in Main Camp, a peaceful rebellion, really, but the peaceful rebellion is the child of the violent protest, as I think you will see. Let me explain. It happens that within Main Camp, the authorities keep a large cage, the size of the biggest room in my family's house in Mazar-e-Sharif, and the cage is made of wire with a wire roof. Within the cage many birds are kept, very many. I have never counted them, but believe me when I say that the birds are many. Some are what I have heard called 'parrots', and they are the most colourful of the birds, red and green and blue and also a yellow colour as bright as the spice that is known as tumeric. Some of the birds are small and yellow, but a different yellow from that of the parrots, and these birds are called canaries, exactly like the canary birds we have in my own land—indeed, just like the canary birds in Gorg Ali's story of the king's son who fell in love with the daughter of a poor man. The biggest of the birds are white with yellow crowns and strong black beaks, and these ones are called Cockies and make sounds like the words they hear, talking sounds. Other birds in the big cage are not so colourful, not so beautiful, but like the colourful birds, they are in a place that makes them unhappy.

Why this cage of birds should be in Woomera has been a puzzle to me. Perhaps keeping birds is a hobby of one of the security guards, or perhaps the people in charge of Woomera think it is pleasant for the refugees to study these birds. But when we study these birds, we have only the one thought, and the thought is this: How wrong to keep these birds from the life they were made by God to live! They fly from one end of the cage to the other, or hang by claws of their feet to the wire and cry out. The birds called Cockies make the loudest sound of all. But now the birds are gone, all of them. I am standing looking at feathers on the floor of the cage, some bright-coloured feathers, many yellow ones, some long, some short. And that is all that is left of the birds. The lock on the door of the cage hangs broken from the wire. I am not the only one gazing at the empty cage. Many of my friends are here, too. We smile at each other. We know who broke the lock and released the birds. We know why the lock was broken, too. We have been told by the security guards that breaking the lock and releasing the birds is 'criminal conduct'. I am sure that is true, and I am sure that I don't approve of 'criminal conduct'. So why am I smiling so much?

10

Gorg Ali and the Watermelons

IN AFGHANISTAN TODAY, it is possible to listen to a story of heartbreak in the morning, hear a more heartbreaking story in the afternoon and in the evening, hear the worst story of all. It is not that Afghanis have chosen a path of suffering out of madness; no, other people have chosen that path for us.

My brother Gorg Ali who was killed by a bullet one dreadful day was one of those people who make the world possible. What I mean is that he was the sort of human being who holds things together, and the opposite of the sort who wrenches things apart. Without people like Gorg Ali, we would be at each other's throats all year long, never knowing that anything else was possible. We would think that bravery meant hitting those we hate with an axe; we would not understand that bravery can be building and making and refusing to lift an axe over our enemies' heads. He was one of those people who *shows*—not as a teacher, but as a person who *shows*. He had no faith in fighting; whether the enemy was Pashtun, Russian, communist or mujahedin mattered little to him. He didn't trust fighting as a way of building, for he'd seen how long fighting can go on, and how reluctant people are to stop once they've started, and how that means little if anything is left standing as the years of fighting pass by.

I don't mean to ask those reading this story to believe that Gorg Ali was a god, or not truly a human being. No, he was as human as anyone; he had to eat to stay alive just like other people, and if he dropped something heavy on his toe by accident, he called out in pain, as we all do. What I am trying to say about him was that he was free of much of the madness that drives other people to do bad things, or things that are bad for the soul. Gorg Ali believed in the earth, as a peasant does. Things made by sweat and toil were important; things made by lying on a sofa all day long were not. Let me put it this way: raising a field of watermelons provided many people with something delicious to eat; writing a speech provided nothing to eat at all. So I would say that my brother Gorg Ali, that beloved man, belonged to the watermelon school of philosophers. I never heard him say so, but I know that if someone had sat with him and spent the whole day explaining what the great philosophers had said about this matter and that matter, Gorg Ali's question would have been: 'Yes, but can you use it to grow watermelons?'

And yet, having said that Gorg Ali was as human as anyone else, I must now tell my readers that my brother was also a person of strange powers. I am thinking especially of his power over snakes.

Afghanistan is like a holiday resort for snakes. They love the climate and bask in the sun whenever they get the chance. The big, black snakes were the ones I saw most of but I'm happy to say I was never bitten by one. Because Afghanis live mostly in the rural areas, snakebite is common enough. Not only humans but animals, too, have to put up with the anger of these fellows. Snakes don't hunt humans, of course; they don't hunt large animals either, only mice and rats. But they attack if you come too close, or if you're tramping about near their nests. They will bite a horse, a donkey, a dog, any creature that they think is a threat. The bite often kills.

And so snakebite is a danger that Afghanis have always had to face and many treatments have been tried over the centuries. Most of these treatments make use of the herbs of the field and some are very reliable. Other treatments make use of the magic that has lived in the land since well before the age of Islam, well before the Shrine of Ali was built in Mazar-e-Sharif.

Gorg Ali was not born with a power over snakes, just as he was not born with his other powers. The powers came to him. And why Gorg Ali and not another? I think it is because these powers of the past only make their home in a man or a woman who can wield them. The powers do not seek out those who are too weak or too silly or too angry or too boastful. In a weak man, the powers would be dangerous, just as they would in a boastful man. And so they live in the earth until they hear the tread of one they trust, and they know they can trust this person by the sound of his feet on the earth. For people walk in many different ways, and the sound they make on the earth is as distinct as the sound of their voice. I know this even though I don't have the power of Gorg Ali. I can tell certain things about a person just by the way he walks. A man who will cheat you reveals his nature with each step. A man you can trust has the walk of a trustworthy man.

And so at a certain time, I think when Gorg Ali was still very young, the powers came out of the soil and rocks of Afghanistan and into his body. It was recognised by everyone in Shar Shar and later by many people in Mazar-e-Sharif that my brother could beguile snakes, and it was accepted as naturally as it was accepted that he was kind and gentle. It was simply something that was true about him. In the summer when snakes move about in the heat people would come running to our house, calling loudly, 'Gorg Ali! Gorg Ali! A demon is in the fields!' and my brother would put down his tools and follow whoever had summoned him to the place where the snake had been seen. Many other people from the village would set aside their work and come to watch. I myself followed the crowd whenever I could. I saw my brother ask where the snake had shown itself. He wanted to know the exact place, not just the general area. I saw him draw a circle on the ground with a stick at that place, and stand in the centre of the circle, and raise his hands in prayer. Then he would spit four times, turning a quarter of the way in the circle each time he spat. Those of us watching glanced about left and right and behind us and before us to see where the snake would emerge from. For we knew that the snake would come to Gorg Ali, perhaps from the cover of the grass and weeds, or from beneath a log, or even from a crack in the earth itself. While we waited, we said nothing. We did not have to remain silent for long. While Gorg Ali stood patiently in the circle, the snake would appear and make straight for the circle and for Gorg Ali himself. And now Gorg Ali would take from his pocket a large piece of cloth that he carried with him at all times in the summer. He would shake the cloth out flat and hold it by the top corners and wave it at the snake. The snake would not hesitate in its approach but would head straight for the cloth and rear and drive its fangs into the fabric and hold on tight. Then it was a simple matter for Gorg Ali to take the snake behind its head and flatten its body on the ground and kill the creature with a blow of his knife. When this was accomplished, the people in the crowd would raise their hands and praise my brother.

Nor were my brother's powers limited to catching the living snakes and putting them to death. He could also revive those who had been bitten by snakes, so long as life was still in the body of the victim. I saw him once go when summoned to the place where a donkey had fallen to its side on the ground with a great swelling on its leg. The swelling meant that the fangs of a snake had pierced its flesh. Gorg Ali took out his knife and wiped the blade once each side of the swelling without splitting the flesh, then he sat back and prayed and spat to the north and south and to the east and west. He waited in silence for a few minutes for the venom and pus to spill from the swelling and run away in thin milky streams. When he saw the venom flow, he knew that his own power had overcome the power of the snake, and the donkey would revive and stand upright again and return to its work. And so it was.

My brother could not pass his powers on to me, but he did teach me how to avoid the black snakes of the fields and the even more dangerous grey snakes of the mountains. When he called me to his side to tell me about snakes, I thought he would reveal the words of his snake prayers or some other spell that would put the snakes under my power. But no, he told me only practical things, sensible things.

'When you see a snake in the mountains,' he told me once, 'do not run up the slope and do not run down the slope. Run sideways across the slope, for a snake cannot gather speed crawling across a slope, it will slip downwards.'

Gorg Ali's powers went far beyond his command of snakes. He knew many things, many remedies. A thousand years ago, before the coming of the Prophet, he would have been the wise man of the village; the person that rulers and peasants alike would have turned to in times of trouble. He may even have been a chieftain but if he was, he would not have been a warlord who rode out on horseback with armed men to conquer and subdue. He was a peaceful man right down to his bones.

※　※　※

One day in the spring of the year 1982 in the Western calendar, Gorg Ali journeyed to our old village of Shar Shar to gather honey from our family's hives. The hives numbered about 200 and were left on land we owned outside the village. The bees made their honey from the wildflowers that grew all over the fields and up into the hills and mountains. The hives had been there for many, many years and the bees knew where their homes were to be found and where the flowers were to be found and so it would have been unwise to move the hives closer to our new home in Mazar-e-Sharif. Besides, a distance such as that between Shar Shar and Mazar-e-Sharif is no big deal in Afghanistan. Gorg Ali went regularly from our new home to the hives without complaint. Once there, he would go from hive to hive, scraping the honey from the sheets of wax and gathering it in drums. This had been one of his jobs since well before I was born and he knew the ways of bees inside out. He knew how much honey the bees would make just by looking across the fields in spring when the wildflowers began to bloom. He knew the quality of the honey to come by the dominance of one type of flower or another.

In the mountain pastures in spring, the wildflowers cover the ground in such numbers that it appears as if a carpet of coloured snow has fallen. I imagine on that day of his death, Gorg Ali would have followed the same plan he'd followed on those occasions when I went with him to the hives. He would first have stood and gazed across the fields of wildflowers and noted the dominance, as ever, of the red poppies and red tulips. And he would have noted, too, that the violets and daisies, purple and yellow, stained the blanket of red in places. He would have looked up to the sky against the peaks of the hills and mountains, so blue that it makes you think, 'Yes, that is where Heaven must be, that is where paradise must be.' Then he would have crossed the streams of freezing silver water that comes down from the mountains in spring, and strode out across the pastures to the hives with the drums for honey and the netting to drape over his face to save him from the bite of the bees.

But on this day, he may have been a little more cautious. Maybe he didn't have as much time to look up to the sky and the mountains as he usually did. The Russians had gone in large numbers to Shar Shar to fight the mujahedin and Gorg Ali would have been aware of the danger. In fighting of the sort that was going on in Afghanistan at this time, neither side gave much thought to civilian casualties. The best a family could hope for if one of their number was killed in the clashes was an apology from whatever commander was responsible.

'Sorry, we didn't mean to kill your son, it was a mistake, really the fault of the people we are fighting.'

But even that was rare. Mostly, the soldiers and tanks simply moved on to the next battlefield unconcerned about the grief they'd left behind. On this day in the spring of 1982, the grief that was left behind was the grief of my family.

I was 12 years old when Gorg Ali made his final visit to the beehives outside Shar Shar. I was working in the rug factory. When I came home from work in the evening two days after Gorg Ali's departure for Shar Shar, my mother called to me from the roof of our house where she had gone to gain a broad view of the road into the city. To reach the roof of the house, you just climbed a tall ladder, and that was what my mother had done, very unwisely, I felt.

'Najaf, have you seen your brother?'

'Which brother?'

'Gorg Ali, have you seen him? He went two days ago to Shar Shar for the honey and hasn't returned. And now comes the news that the Russians have gone to Shar Shar to fight. I am full of fear for him.'

When my mother told me of the Russians going to Shar Shar, I too felt worried. But I didn't say anything of that sort to my mother. Instead I tried to comfort her, in the way that we do when we see someone is afraid.

'Surely he has found some business to do in Shar Shar,' I said. 'Surely he has been delayed. But he will return.'

'All about my heart I have such fear,' said my mother.

'Come down from there,' I called to my mother. 'Come into the house. Gorg Ali will return.'

My mother started down the ladder, but the burden of her aged body together with the distraction of Gorg Ali's absence must have caused her to miss a step and she fell heavily with a loud scream onto the wooden surround of our well. I ran to her and struggled to heave her inside, supporting her whole weight. It was obvious to me that she was badly hurt. With my arms around her, I could feel the thud of her heartbeat and I was terrified that the beating would suddenly stop. The blood from her gashes seeped through the fabric of my trousers and onto my flesh.

My sister and sisters-in-law helped her into bed, and there she lay for the whole night in great pain, although the pain in her heart would have been greater than the pain of her bruised bones. When she was not crying out in pain, she was praying for the safe return of her eldest son and child. 'Ah, God, what becomes of me means nothing, but my son, my son!'

In my bed, I prayed too with all my might. I told myself that he was surely well and I would see him the next day, but that didn't stop me from imploring God, if it should be His will, to restore my brother to those that loved him and depended on him.

It was not to be, alas. We did not hear any news of Gorg Ali the next day, nor for 15 more days. The fighting near Shar Shar made it impossible for anyone to go and look for Gorg Ali. Finally, a half-brother of ours, Zahir, went to Shar Shar to search for Gorg Ali. By this time, the Russians had withdrawn, having accomplished nothing, and the mujahedin had withdrawn, and they too had accomplished nothing. Zahir walked along the route to the hives that Gorg Ali would have taken, and on the way he saw the signs of the battle that had been fought:

113

shell craters, and a few buildings destroyed and still smoking, and blackened grass and pasture, and the wrappers of food rations that the Russians had thrown away as they made their way forward or backwards, depending on how the battle went. He scanned the fields with his sure eyesight and for some time found no sign of Gorg Ali. But as he approached closer to the fields of hives where the poppies and tulips still stood, he glimpsed something ahead and to his sorrow what he had glimpsed became a man, and the man became Gorg Ali, felled by a single bullet.

When my brother's body was found, we did not know immediately. We'd had no news of the outcome of Zahir's mission. We had passed the hours in great hope of a happy ending to this day. But when we saw Zahir approaching along the road, our hopes died on the spot. He came stooped over with grief, looking not at us but at a place beyond us. When he came closer and could no longer avoid our eyes, he lifted his arms and let them fall, again and again. Then he put one hand over his own face, as if afraid of the story his own grief would reveal.

My mother struggled to the road, the pain of what she now knew she would hear overwhelming the pain of her torn legs and bruised bones, while I took the hem of my shirt in my mouth and bit it hard to keep from screaming aloud.

When Zahir reached our house, the sorrow on his face showed us, if we needed any further proof, that Gorg Ali was dead.

Losing Gorg Ali was, for me and for my brothers and sisters, like losing our father all over again. His body was recovered three days later by Zahir and my uncle when the fighting had moved away from Shar Shar completely. We buried Gorg

Ali outside of Shar Shar and mourned him according to the traditions of the Hazara, and according to our hearts.

The loss we felt was all the more dreadful because we knew that a bad time was coming for our country and we would be without the man who had guided us through the awful times we had already endured. We were expecting fighting all over Afghanistan.

Now, it was true that we were used to the fighting, but by 1982 it was obvious to everyone that the bitterness of the conflict between the communist government and the mujahedin was going to tear the country into pieces. My land of Afghanistan is not a land of brief wars. A war may last 50 years without it being thought especially long. In this war, some of us had expected that the mujahedin would take over some sections of the country and reinforce their bases there, restricting the fighting to provinces in the south and the north-east along the Pakistan border. The communist government with the help of the Russians would control most of Afghanistan, including Kabul. But what we came to understand was that the mujahedin, an alliance of about a dozen small armies, had the better strategy—a guerrilla strategy—while the government had the better armaments. So the mujahedin would eventually win, but the Russian armaments of the government would make sure that the mujahedin's victory would take a long time. And when the mujahedin won their final victory, that was when the real trouble would start.

Let me explain.

'Mujahedin' is just a term that means 'freedom fighters' or 'holy warriors'. Anyone who takes up arms against a government can call himself a mujahedin. But Afghanis didn't take up arms individually; they did so in groups, according to their ethnic origin and their region. Afghanistan has always been a tribal country made up of hundreds of regions each under the control of a different chieftain. Each chieftain is expected to guard the interests of his tribe, above all else. Of course, the chieftains know that they are all Afghanis and they know that when all of the Afghanis are put together, they become part of the nation of Afghanistan. But the chieftains never forget where they come from, and what their real task is in life. They will unite to fight a common enemy (such as the communists and the Russians, or earlier on, the British, or even earlier still, an older generation of Russians) but they might be fighting amongst themselves at the same time, making sure that they lose no ground to their neighbours. And when they eventually defeat the common enemy, who is to say which chieftain is to be the Chief of Chiefs? Maybe the chieftains will come to an agreement and install one man as the Chief of Chiefs, but that man will need to look over his shoulder for the rest of his life, because there is certain to be another chieftain who wants his job.

Although the chieftains of Afghanistan are always prepared to fight for their territory, and although skirmishes go on all the time, for long periods a type of balance is achieved. And this balance is something Afghanis can live with. It's not exactly peace, and it's not exactly war. If this balance is upset and one chieftain is attacked by another and allies are called in, then the fighting spreads and spreads. And that is exactly what we could all see happening—a big battle that would go on and on until the balance was found again.

In our house, we went about as if a big black cloud was sitting right on top of us. We all had our work to do, but in the pit of our stomachs we feared that the cloud above us would break with a sound like a bomb going off and we would be swept away in the deluge. Our neighbours all had the same wary look as us. They, too, had noticed the big black cloud. But in such situations, you must go on working steadily. I went six days a week to the carpet factory and learned a little more with each passing month. My passion for my craft grew more intense the more I learned. When I was rolling the skeins of wool, I watched the students making the borders of the rugs on the loom. When I was at last permitted to work at the loom, I watched the teacher creating the patterns. I thought to myself, 'Whatever I learn, I will not forget, and all the learning will build upon itself. Then the day will come when I will be the teacher, when I will be the master, and that will be my work in this world. To make rugs. To make beautiful rugs.'

✳ ✳ ✳

My brother Abdul Ali took over the care of the hives at Shar Shar, without neglecting his other jobs. Working so hard did not improve his temper. Because I was now my mother's second oldest son, more responsibility settled onto my shoulders too. I had more chores to attend to; more to worry about. I could feel the days of my boyhood receding further and further into memory, like the sound of lovely music growing more distant. I found myself looking at the world in the way an adult does. I worried about the weather, I worried about the Russians, I worried about the mujahedin, I worried about money. I worried about Gorg Ali's children, too: my nieces and nephews. Once, I was their playmate, now I was expected to be a stern uncle, reminding them to attend to their schoolwork and their chores. I particularly worried about my younger brother Rosal Ali, who lived his life as if he intended to become a circus clown. He seemed to have no idea of the seriousness of things. He laughed, he joked, he ran away to play with his friends. From the age of ten, he worked as a carpenter's apprentice, making wooden boxes and crates, but it was common for him to simply forget that he had a job at all and stroll off into the city to amuse himself. Often I got fed up with him and shouted at him, just as Abdul Ali sometimes shouted at me. It was as if I were in training to become another Abdul Ali. I recall a day when Rosal Ali did something that really got under my skin. What it was, I can't remember, but it would have resulted in me having to do extra work. When I found him, I shouted at him at the top of my voice.

'Why are you so stupid? Why can't you listen when you are told things? God Himself looks down on you with disgust! He wonders why He made you to begin with!'

Rosal Ali could see how angry I was and turned and ran. But I had blocked his exit from the house, intending to box his ears, and so he ran to a room with a bolt on the door and locked himself in. This made me angrier than ever. I ran to the window of the room that he'd locked himself in and screamed at him to open the door. But he just stood there, trembling and grinning at the same time, as if he were frightened of me but still saw the funny side of me shrieking at him through the glass of the window. I smashed the window with my fist in my determination to get at him and the glass sliced deeply into my hand. Blood ran over my hand and down my arm and splattered on the ground. The cut didn't stop me; I still attempted to reach the lock on the window to open it. But then I saw just how much blood was escaping from the wound, and I became scared. My mother came running and screamed aloud for help. Eventually, the doctor in Mazar-e-Sharif closed the wound with a dozen stitches. Rosal Ali seemed ashamed of having been the cause of my wound, but defiant at the same time.

A wound on the hand is the last thing I needed as a rugmaker. My hands were tools. But I still went to work at the rug factory, managing as best I could. There were no unemployment benefits in Afghanistan at that time; no sickness pensions. As I sat working at the loom, I wondered if I would ever enjoy a happy, carefree day again. Was this what life was? Just one catastrophe after another? I had to tell myself, 'Najaf, happier times will come. Be patient. Watch your temper. Happier times will come.'

Alas, those happier times were a long way away. For every year that passed on the calendar, I felt that I had aged two years. At the rate I was going, I would be an old man with a white beard before I was 20.

11

Love and Music

A HUMAN HEART is a chamber in which great forces of energy seethe and hiss and erupt. When we see the heavy black clouds of a thunderstorm gather in the sky above the mountains, we know that we will soon see lightning flashing in the heavens, and we will hear great crashes of thunder that make windows shake in their frames, and we will stand back under what shelter we can find and watch the rain that has been flung down to the earth to boil in pools and raise the level of streams and run in torrents over the fields. We will stare in amazement at the violence of the skies, and think, 'Ah, what in God's creation can equal this?' But in the human heart, such passions rage that the lightning and thunder and the torrents of the storm would themselves stand back in awe. In the heart of the poor man who stabbed needles through his lips, such a passion was set loose. But I see other passions strike their own lightning in Woomera, although they are not as violent and do not lead to the shedding of blood.

I have a good friend in Woomera who came with me to Main Camp. His name is Abbas, a fellow countryman. Abbas is a master of the musical instrument we call a tula in Afghanistan—an instrument played like a flute by blowing across the opening, and also played like a recorder by blowing into the opening. The music of the tula is like the language that angels would speak, if we could hear them. Abbas sits cross-legged with his tula outside his dormitory and plays for the pleasure of playing. People gather around, men and women, and listen as if enchanted. They call out compliments to Abbas, and praise God for having given this gift to him. With his music, Abbas restores some peace in a place where people sorely need relief from worry.

Even when he is not playing the tula, Abbas attracts a crowd. He is a man of humour, and people like to be close to him. I do not mean that Abbas is a clown. No, it is just that humour flavours everything he has to say, like the sauce that we add to a dish to enhance its taste. He can't help it. Humour is in his heart, and whenever he speaks, he speaks from his heart.

One morning in Main Camp, Abbas calls to me as I am driving along in a vehicle that we call 'the mule'—a small truck that we use for carrying cartons from the stores in Main Camp to the mess. I am not an accomplished driver, but it is a simple matter to steer the mule. Driving along on this day, as I say, Abbas has stopped me and asks me to pay close attention to what he has to tell me. He is not quite his normal, happy self, I can see that. Something powerful is working in him; something that has made his eyes sorrowful and his broad smiling face a little drawn. He gets me to step out of the mule and sit with him a little away from where people can see us. I am worried, as well as mystified, because this is not normal Abbas behaviour. He is never secretive. In fact, he lives his whole life in the open, in front of everyone.

'Najaf, you are my dear friend, do you agree?'

'Of course! How can you ask?'

'I have something to tell you. And I have a great favour to ask you.'

'Anything.'

Abbas pauses and looks around, as if he fears that we are being studied by a secret policeman. He puts his hand in his hair and rubs his scalp, moaning faintly.

'Here's the truth. I have fallen in love.'

Now, it was not my intention, but when Abbas says, 'I have fallen in love,' I laugh out loud. It is not a cruel laugh, but instead a laugh of astonishment. Abbas frowns at me, and puts a finger to his lips.

'Shhh!'

'Sorry, sorry. I didn't mean that.'

'You think this is amusing? You think I enjoy this?'

'No, forgive me, Abbas. You are my dear friend.'

Abbas studies my face closely, as if trying to decide if his trust is misplaced. For my part, I attempt to look as sincere and as serious as a mullah.

'I say again. I have fallen in love.'

This time, I pass the test. I nod my head like a holy man and put my hand to my chin.

'Indeed,' I say.

'You know the woman I am about to speak of,' says Abbas,

and he gives another small groan.

'Indeed,' I say again, still trying to sound very serious. It is not at all surprising that I know the woman that Abbas has fallen in love with, because I know all the women and all the men and all the children that he is likely to come into contact with. But then a thought occurs to me that makes me grip my friend's shoulder and whisper in alarm, 'An Australian? Have you fallen in love with a woman from the office?'

'An Australian? No!' says Abbas. 'What do I know of Australian women? Be sensible, Najaf!'

'I am sorry. Just for a minute, I was concerned.'

'Have you seen me play the tula?' he asks, and this is such a foolish question because everyone gathers to hear him play the tula.

But I say, 'I have. Of course.'

'Do you know why I play the tula?'

'Because…' I begin, then stop to reflect. 'Because you can?' I say.

'No! Are you listening to me at all? Has your new responsibility made you deaf?'

Abbas means the driving of the mule.

'No, no, no. Please go on.'

'I play the tula,' he says, 'for her.'

'For her?'

'Yes.'

'For who?'

'For her.'

'The woman you are talking about?'

Abbas walks away three or four steps, then walks back. His face is full of a strange sort of anger.

'Yes, yes! Who do you think? Kandhi Hazara?'

'My apologies,' I say, and I add the word that I have been using to show how serious I am, even though there is no sensible reason for me to use it just at this moment: 'Indeed.' It is very plain to me that my wonderful friend, so full of life and humour, has gone mad.

'She watches me play,' says Abbas. 'She listens. There is joy in her eyes.'

I think of saying, 'There is joy in everybody's eyes when they hear you play,' but instead I simply say, 'Indeed' again.

'And,' says Abbas, 'I ask you to carry to her my offer of marriage.'

'Really?'

'Yes!'

'Then of course. Who is she?'

Abbas again makes an agonised expression, as if the woman he has fallen in love with radiates light like a great fire in the desert at night; a beacon that any man who is not blind must have noticed. He leans close to me and seizes my arm. His grip is painful. He whispers a name.

'Go!' he says. 'Go!'

'I have to deliver all this to the mess.'

'Deliver it! Then go!'

I head back to the mule, but Abbas takes big strides and stops me. 'Don't say it is me!' he says.

'What?' Now I am certain he has gone mad.

'Just say a friend of yours. Do you understand?'

'Just say a friend?'

'Yes! Do you understand?'

'Okay.'

The woman Abbas has named is truly a great beauty. She is not a mere girl, but a grown woman, very intelligent and sophisticated. In the country she came from, she was a doctor. I know her quite well. She often wears an amused expression, but not quite the same amused expression that Abbas wears. I would guess that she knows she is beautiful, but does not count that as being of much importance. In my heart, I fear that Abbas has set his sights too high. I do not mean that the woman would look down on him, but probably she expects to marry a professional man, rather than a travelling musician. Still, with women you can never be certain. They sometimes think in ways that men cannot fathom. They are not as predictable as men.

After I unload all the cartons from the mule, I return the vehicle to the depot and go directly to the room where the woman is staying. She has a room to herself, as a few of the single women do, perhaps because the larger rooms for women are filled with mothers who have children around them all day long.

I knock on the door, then stand back a little way. The lady comes to the door, looking surprised. I have never come to call on her privately before. Such a visit from a man to the room of a single woman is very unusual.

'Najaf? Has something happened?'

'Yes. May I talk with you about a very delicate matter?'

She looks at me with her head on the side, as if I am having a joke with her—a joke she doesn't understand.

'Truly?' she says.

'Truly.'

I do not go into her room, but rather she comes out and stands with me in the open. It is important that people see that we are not attempting a secret meeting. I tell her, very gently, that the matter I wish to speak of concerns love.

She says, 'Is it that you wish to marry me?' She is smiling when she says this; the smile of someone who is a little puzzled at what she has heard, although not displeased.

I shake my head and hold up my hands.

'No, no, not me but my friend.'

I tell her of Abbas's love for her, without naming Abbas. I tell her of his proposal of marriage. And just as I myself did when Abbas first spoke of love to me, she laughs. And just like me, she seems a little embarrassed by her laugh, and repents of it.

'Who is this friend?' she asks. I really wish to say my friend's name, because she might think it is still me who is courting her.

'A friend of great talent,' I say.

'Greater than your own?' she asks. She is teasing me, I realise.

'Much greater.'

'A genius, then?'

'In his way.'

She becomes serious again. I can tell by her expression that she knows it is Abbas I am talking about. My speaking of great talent has given him away.

She says that she must say no. She has two brothers in Sydney. It is they who will decide whom she marries. I cannot tell if she would overrule her brothers if she truly loved Abbas, or if she sincerely feels that she isn't free to choose for herself. Nevertheless, we part in a friendly way, with a smile, and I return to Abbas.

People who are waiting on good news cannot always tell if you are bringing the good news they crave to hear. People who

ABOVE
The house in the village of Shar Shar where Najaf was born.

BELOW
Najaf's nephew who lost his two legs when he stepped on a roadside bomb near his village.

ABOVE
The medical clinic in the village of Shar Shar which has only one doctor and a medical assistant to treat the entire community.

BELOW
The poor quality road between Mazar-e-Sharif and Shar Shar. The tangi – Afghan word meaning 'archway' – was man-made centuries ago.

ABOVE
Najaf's family house in Mazar-e-Sharif which was damaged
by a rocket attack that killed 2 family members and seriously
injured Najaf.

BELOW
The Blue Mosque of Mazar-e-Sharif, Holy Shrine of Ali,
cousin and son-in-law of the prophet Mohammed.

ABOVE
Najaf in 2004 in
his rug shop in
Melbourne,
Australia, before
he was reunited
with his family.
Photo: Jeremy Wells

LEFT
Najaf with his
daughter Maria after
their Citizenship
ceremony in
April 2007 at the
Malvern Town Hall,
Melbourne, Australia.
Photo: Joseph Feil

fear bad news can tell in an instant if what they fear is about to be confirmed. And so it is with Abbas. He glances at me, frowns, looks down at the ground, then raises his head again and smiles with such sadness that I feel tears swell in my eyes.

'No?' says Abbas.

'No,' I say.

'It doesn't matter.'

'Her brothers in Sydney must choose her husband. They probably have someone already.'

'It doesn't matter.'

Abbas smiles as broadly as he ever has. Indeed, he seems relieved, in a way. But at the same time, he cannot hide the fact that his heart is broken. His lips trembles a little as he smiles. His eyes are dark, instead of sparkling as they normally are.

'I'm sorry,' I say.

'But she doesn't know it was me?' says Abbas. 'You kept my secret?'

'She knows nothing,' I lie.

'I can keep playing for her, then,' says Abbas. A little light returns to his eyes. 'At least that. And that is a lot. Yes, with that I can be happy.'

'Truly?'

'Truly. Truly. And Najaf, my great thanks.'

The next time Abbas plays, the lady he loves is not amongst the crowd. She is not there the next day, either. I go to her room again and ask her not to avoid Abbas; for if she does, she will destroy what is left of his heart.

When Abbas plays the tula the following day, the woman joins the crowd, and listens.

12

Two Red Pills

I SPOKE EARLIER in my story of the mujahedin rocket that destroyed my family's house, killed my younger brother Rosal Ali, and my brother-in-law, and drove shrapnel into my leg putting me into hospital. But I didn't mention that my family's house was the only one destroyed that night; that my brother and brother-in-law were the only people killed by the rocket, and that my mother and Abdul Ali and I were the only ones injured by it. Just one rocket, and fate guided it to me. I didn't know until two days after the explosion that the Mazari family had been the only family to suffer that night. When I was told, I wept. It was not that I wished to hear that many other people had been killed or wounded; no, I was glad that the damage had not been worse. The reason I wept was that I thought God had chosen my family for special suffering. In little more than a year, we had lost Gorg Ali, and then another relative, a favourite of my mother's, murdered in his market garden; then my brother-in-law, and Rosal Ali.

The shrapnel had done terrible damage to the calf of my left leg. It was necessary for me to remain in hospital for three months while the wound was treated. The flesh of my leg had been torn open in the way that a plough cuts through the earth, leaving a pile of freshly-turned soil on either side of a trench. The doctors had sewn the living flesh back into the trench after cutting away the dead flesh. But the wound was not healing, and the pain it caused made me gasp and sweat and grit my teeth all through the day and night.

Around me, in the crowded ward of the hospital lay people wounded in other battles, the victims of other catastrophes. And this was a civilian hospital—none of the people who groaned in pain or prayed to God for relief were soldiers. For Afghanis, warfare had become a disaster so common that it was useless to think of it as something that could be avoided; it was more like earthquakes and floods and plague—catastrophes that you had to live with because they could not be controlled.

If I could have made my pain go away just by wishing, then of course I would have wished it away. But if I'd had just one wish and so had to choose between getting rid of the pain, or regaining the use of my leg, I would have said, 'The pain I will endure, but let me keep my leg.' I did not want to be a cripple for life. I have seen many cripples in Afghanistan. Legs are torn away; hands, whole arms, or sometimes all the limbs, leaving just the body. In a land of explosions, you see everything that explosions can do to human beings. And my land is a difficult land to live in without two strong legs. It is not a land of leisure, and it is not a land of handsome pensions. It is a land of work. As I grew from a small boy into a bigger boy and into my teenage years, I knew one thing above all others: that my life would be a life of work. Without my left leg, my chances of making a proper living would be about zero. I would be a burden not only to myself, but to my family. So each day, and many times each day, I worried about my leg. I worried that the doctor would come and remove the dressings and study the wound and shake his head and say, 'Najaf, be brave when you hear what I must tell you. Your leg is to be amputated.'

Three weeks after the explosion of the rocket, the doctor remained optimistic, even though the wound refused to close. The doctor had seen many such wounds and knew what he was talking about, so I took comfort in his optimism. But after four weeks, and then five weeks, I could see my own fears reflected in the expression of the doctor when he peered at the naked wound. He was not so optimistic as he had been. He told me that the wound was more difficult than most because it was a shrapnel wound.

'The metal case of the rocket is coated with chemicals,' he said. 'The metal cuts the flesh, and the chemicals burn it. Do you feel a pain such as would trouble you if you were burnt?'

'Yes,' I told him. 'A burning pain, certainly.'

'We will wait and see,' said the doctor. 'We may have to operate again.'

All through the days and the nights, I listened to the cries and groans of those in the ward and even from further away. Most of these people had as much to worry about as me. Some had already said goodbye to their legs. After seven weeks, I ceased to hear the cries of those around me, just as they ceased to hear my cries, I have no doubt. The sounds of anguish became background noise.

When you are forced to remain in bed for a long time at a stretch, you might begin to use some of that time to think about life and God and the things that are of the most importance. I attempted to profit from this period of being bedridden by thinking of such matters of importance—at least, I did so when the pain was not too great and my anxiety was not overwhelming. 'Najaf,' I thought, 'if you cannot use your legs, at least use your mind.' And so I would reflect on great matters. I would think of God's creation in all of its wonder and beauty, and of God's plan for me, and of the strange ways in which that plan was unfolding. But there was a problem for me, which other people in my position may also have encountered: the more I thought about great and important matters, the more I found myself, after about five minutes, wondering about things that were not nearly so great and important. Why have snakes no legs? How is it possible to see through certain solid things, like glass? Why is water colourless? How can flowers of the most brilliant colours bloom from dull brown earth? Whenever I found myself puzzling over these humble questions, I would shake my head and attempt to return to the great and important questions once more. But alas!—after another five minutes, I would be back with the legless snakes, or with that other baffling question: what was invented first, the hammer or the nail? After many fruitless attempts to understand life and God's plans, I realised that my brain could only enjoy such questioning if my hands had work to do. Otherwise, what was the use of knowing the answers to great questions? But at least this attempt to see into the mystery of things had one benefit, for I realised that a man is not what he thinks, not what he says, but what he does with his hands and legs and with his heart.

I had visitors each day. Many of my uncles and cousins and in-laws came to see me, also my mother whenever she could spare time from her burden of work in the house, and my brother, Abdul Ali. Most Afghanis with grown-up brothers and sisters receive a great number of visitors in hospital, for Afghani families are like a rug or a runner that unrolls down a corridor past the doors of many rooms. My father had more than one wife, and so each wife multiplied my store of relatives. My brothers and sisters had children of their own, too, and some of them came to see me. My visitors sat on my bed or on a bench against the wall. Often, there was not a great deal of conversation. A few things were said, yes, but there was no chatter that went on for the whole length of the visit. Afghanis do not feel awkward if there is a lull in the conversation. The important thing is that the visitor has brought himself to your bedside. He is not required to entertain you, and you are not expected to entertain him. What conversation there was had only two themes: wishes for my full recovery and a head-shaking amazement that a single rocket had found the roof of our house rather than the much vaster, unhoused area to each side.

After three months of lying in bed, my left leg was sealed in a cast, crutches were provided for me, and I was sent home.

The house was in the process of being rebuilt by Abdul Ali. Because Afghan houses are not so divided inside as Western houses with walls separating off numerous rooms, the repairs soon restored enough of the place to provide shelter. Large sheets of clear plastic replaced the glass windows, every one of which had been shattered into fragments. I was welcomed back into the house with as much rejoicing as if I'd returned from a long journey to some dangerous land. Holding myself upright on my crutches, I gazed around picking out points where evidence of the explosion was still visible. Walls pock-marked by flying fragments of glass made me think of walls against which people have been shot by firing squads. Anything that showed the impact of the explosion made me feel dizzy and ill. I was, in truth, still full of the fear of that night when the rocket landed. As I looked about me, how could I say that another such rocket would not seek out this house, even within seconds? When the body has suffered great harm, it remembers forever. It does not say, 'But it would be almost impossible for such a thing to happen again.' It says, instead, 'The next rocket is on its way.'

Cripples in poor lands like mine are like the sparrows of a city. We search for crumbs that have fallen into cracks, then retrieve them one at a time. A whole day's searching for crumbs will barely yield a sparrow enough for half a meal, and so it was with me. I purchased second-hand woollen garments from the bazaar with money I had saved from rug-making before the night of the rocket, picked the garments apart and set to work on the floor of the house with a crocheting board to make socks. My injured leg in its cast was stretched out straight on the floor. When I'd produced a few pairs of socks, I hobbled on my crutches to a street corner close to our wrecked house, laid down a kilim to sit on and set to work again with the crochet board and wool. The pairs of socks I'd completed were neatly placed in a row before me. People stopped to study my wares, sometimes finding in their purse the few coins needed to purchase what I had made. Often, those who stopped would simply make conversation.

'What has brought you to this sorry pass, you poor fellow?'

'A rocket.'

'So, a rocket you say? Russian?'

'Who knows? We think it was mujahedin.'

'Those boys should take more care. Will you recover?'

'God willing.'

'I will recall you in my prayers. I wish I had the coins for a pair of your socks, but alas, food must come first.'

'I understand.'

When you are a cripple, you notice for the first time how many people are not. Of course, in Afghanistan as I have said, legs are lost all the time and each day you will see a dozen people hobbling on crutches, or walking stiffly on a cheap artificial leg. But these are not the people who make the greatest impression on you. Sitting on my kilim, I watched countless boys of my age walking nimbly down the street, or even running. I thought to myself how little I had valued the use of two good legs when I had them. It seemed amazing to me that I had not blessed God each day for the use of my legs. It made me think of the other parts of me that I should value highly: my hands, my brain. But instead of counting my blessings, I remained downcast and watched jealously as those on two strong legs hurried by. I wanted to shout out at times, 'Hey you, pay more attention to me! You might be doing my job one day!'

Each week, I hobbled to the hospital to have my leg looked at and to have dressings replaced. Each week, the doctor pursed his lips as he gazed at the wound, or took his chin in his hand and wrinkled his brow. What I wanted to say to the doctor was, 'Just fix it! Fix it today! Are you a doctor or a baker?' I remained respectful in what I said, naturally, but my despondency was growing deeper. At home, my family was beginning to think that I was to be their burden for the rest of my life. They did not say so, nor would they have resented me being a burden, but little by little, I could see that their attitude was changing from hope for me, to acceptance of my state.

The doctor at the hospital proposed a new operation. He said that fabric from my pyjama trousers was still embedded in my leg and that only when the fabric was cleaned out would my wound truly heal. I shrugged my shoulders at this news. There seemed no end to the reasons the doctor could give for my wound remaining so raw. I went to the hospital on the day appointed for the operation with my head on my chest. Just as I was standing in the room outside the operating theatre waiting for instructions, I was jolted fully awake by the words of the female nurse: 'Please remove all of your garments,' she said.

'I beg your pardon?'

'Please remove all of your garments.'

'When?'

'Now.'

'Now?'

'Of course.'

'But where will you be, miss?'

'Here.'

I could feel my face and indeed the whole of my torso turning red with embarrassment. Was this the sort of request that was common in places where female nurses worked? I was horrified.

'Miss, please excuse me, but I cannot undress if you remain here.'

'Pff! Nonsense!'

'I'm serious.'

The nurse rolled her eyes and pulled a sheet from the bed for me to wrap around myself. I wrapped myself up as tightly as an Egyptian mummy, in more pain from my embarrassment than from the wound in my leg. I realised that I was in many ways still a village boy, a shepherd, but I couldn't help that. A world in which a female nurse would stand by while a boy undressed? Was this an idea introduced by the communists, who didn't know right from wrong? Then even as I painfully worked my clothes off under the cover of the sheet, I realised that on the night of the rocket attack when I was first brought to the hospital, I was not conscious. Maybe the female nurses— maybe this very nurse!—saw my naked body. The thought brought on a fresh flush of embarrassment. For a moment, this incident that I could not even remember—being seen naked by female nurses—seemed to me an even worse catastrophe than the wound itself.

The operation was not such a great success. Certainly, the pain was relieved slightly, but the wound was still unhealed. By this time, my despondency was at its worst. What else could be done for me? I'd had a second operation, I'd had medicine, I'd had months of resting the leg to allow it to heal, and all of this had gained me very, very little. The few coins I could make crocheting socks barely supported me. Any expense that my tiny income would not cover—such as medicines and clothes—had to be borrowed from Abdul Ali, to my great embarrassment. Abdul Ali was himself almost a pauper. As the oldest surviving brother of the family, the expense of rebuilding the house fell on him. There was no compensation from the government for the destruction of the house, and in Afghanistan, insurance is no more than a mysterious arrangement that people in fat, wealthy countries can afford. Abdul Ali had also to meet the expense of the funerals of Gorg Ali, then of Rosal Ali. In Afghanistan, the two events that can leave you with empty pockets are marriages and burials. Both cost a fortune, but people dare not hold back when marriages and funerals come around, or else they will be whispered about until the end of their days. People would say, 'Friend, did you hear of so-and-so? His family buried him like a beggar. A disgrace and an insult to Heaven!' So when it came time for me to beg a few coins from Abdul Ali, I felt sick with shame. And this state of affairs was to go on and on! I was sure I would not be able to bear it. I would go crazy.

But I did not go crazy.

One day, returning from the hospital in a taxi after a visit to have my wound studied, the taxi driver began to question me about my leg.

'How did this come about?' he asked, and I told him.

'Surely you will be a whole person again with time?' he said.

'It has been a year,' I said.

'Whoo! A year! I have known people to recover from the loss of two legs in a year! Something is amiss.'

Did I need a taxi driver to tell me this? Of course something was wrong.

We drove along in silence for a few minutes, then the taxi driver said, 'I have the solution.'

'Don't give me hope unless you are serious,' I said. 'God is watching.'

The taxi driver was offended. He wasn't to know that I had waited and prayed through so many nights and days for hope to come to life in my heart again.

'Please yourself,' he said, showing that his feelings were hurt. 'But your long face and ruined leg will win you few friends in life.'

I apologised immediately. 'My manners are almost as ruined as my leg,' I said. 'Forgive me, sir. Tell me what you were about to say.'

The taxi driver allowed me to sit through a few minutes of silence. Then without warning he became the cheerful, talkative person he'd been when I'd first struggled into his vehicle.

'You see,' he said, 'you don't need a leg doctor. You need a brain doctor.'

He tapped his forehead with two fingers. I thought, 'I shouldn't have listened. He's insane.'

'My brain is undamaged,' I said. 'Thank you for your suggestion.'

'No, no. I don't mean a brain doctor who looks into your skull. This is a different doctor. Believe me, the man works miracles.'

I accepted a piece of paper from the taxi driver with the address of the doctor who made miracles happen written on it. And because I had nothing else and no one else to turn to, I went to see the brain doctor, who was in fact a psychiatrist.

The psychiatrist sat behind his desk looking like a holy man and acting like a holy man. As soon as I saw him, I repented all my doubts. He looked at me as if he already knew everything about me, every fact, every thought that had ever formed in my mind. His face was as calm and as still as a portrait. But at the same time—and this will sound very strange—he seemed impatient. When I began in an awkward way to tell him my story, he looked away and yawned. He kept looking away for the whole time I spoke. I don't think he heard a word I said to him.

When I finished speaking, he opened a drawer in his desk and took out two red pills. He did not take them from a packet or from a jar, he simply took them from the drawer.

'Take these,' he said. 'One today when you get home. One tomorrow.'

I began to wonder if both the taxi driver and this strange brain doctor had run away from a mental hospital. But the brain doctor seemed so sure of what he said and his expression was so fixed and calm that I accepted the two red pills, which cost me next to nothing, then went home.

I took the first red pill straight away. When I went to bed that night, my leg was still causing me as much pain and discomfort as ever. But when I woke up, the burning feeling had faded greatly, to my amazement. So I took the second pill. By the next day, the burning sensation had disappeared completely. I waited anxiously to see if the pain would return, but it did not. And the wound began to heal itself steadily.

I thought: Yes, this is a miracle. But is the miracle in the two pills or in the brain doctor's calm expression? If two such pills could fix me, surely they could cure everyone in Afghanistan who needed healing. Why were such pills not famous up and down the length of the land? Why did I have to stumble on a talkative taxi driver before I could find a cure for my wound? I felt as if I was in a story in a book; a story like those that poor people tell of a stranger who comes to a house of illness and despair in the middle of the night, drinks a glass of water from the family well and leaves a blessing behind that brings joy and health to the family.

I worried that thinking too much about the miracle would make it wither away. I said to myself, 'Najaf, if a man is dying in the desert then finds a well where no well should exist, would the man not be a fool if he refused to drink the water? If the man survives but worries that what saved his life was an illusion, his worries are nonsense.' So I ceased to worry and enjoyed my recovery. I returned to rug-making. Whenever I thought over the next few months of the two red pills that cured me, I only smiled and murmured, 'God provides.'

13

Apple

THE LONGER I REMAIN in Main Camp, the more aware I become that life is a force that never takes a holiday, never rests. At first I thought that life had more or less come to a halt in Woomera, or that life had paused, just as there may be an enforced pause in a long journey when the bus breaks down, or when you come to a river that is swollen with spring rain and cannot be crossed until it returns to normal. Woomera was, so I thought, no more than a place of waiting and of watching for the river to recede. Life would begin again when the journey resumed. But now when I look about, I see that all the events that take place in the world outside Woomera happen here, too. Children are born; men and women fall in love; great passions are roused by the struggle for equality; people of honour attempt to spread their influence and bring about peace; people of ill will attempt to subdue those who resist their plans. Here in Woomera, we have all the members of the human family, for better or worse.

Imagine that all the people in Australia should disappear one day; taken away by strangers from the planet of Mars in big spaceships, leaving only the refugees of Woomera behind. This is quite impossible, I know, but just for argument's sake, imagine it. What would become of the refugees of Woomera? I'll tell you. With the passing of time, the refugees would become the new generation of Australians. And all the passions and hopes we have brought with us would be there, ready to flourish in this new land. We have artists here amongst us; we have musicians; we have mechanics, carpenters, scientists, rugmakers; we have people with good business brains; we have philosophers, engineers; we have teachers, holy men, poets. We have women who know how to raise children, men who know how to be good fathers. And we have scoundrels and thugs and criminals and bullies, too—that is only to be expected. We have everything and everyone; the world packed into a small parcel.

If we Woomerians had to make a new Australia, we would do a good job—not a better job than the real Australians have done, but almost as good, and maybe a bit different. We would make small towns and big cities and hospitals and schools and universities and long straight roads with white lines down the middle (Australians make excellent roads, I've noticed) and lolly shops and ice-cream parlours, parks and factories. We would make everything that is here already. And we would make mosques and churches and synagogues. We would make laws, too; fine laws, like the ones the Australians already have. And the scoundrels and liars and thugs amongst us would meet the fate of all such people and end up in prison after a very fair trial. We would fall in love and marry and have children. We would make things of great beauty to go into museums. We would make the most beautiful rugs in the world, for example. Because when we came here across the desert and across the sea, we brought with us all that would be needed stored in our hearts and minds and souls. That is what I understand now as I walk about Main Camp.

The passions that we have brought with us have touched me in a strange way. Let me tell you a story of passions in which I am one of the two main characters. But before I begin, let me remind my readers that I came to Australia a married man and a father. Hakima, my wife, and Maria, my daughter, are awaiting me in a safe place within Pakistan. Not one hour in a day passes without my thoughts turning to them. I send them my love in whispers when I lie in the dark of the dormitory. I name them in my prayers when I kneel to honour God. They are as much a part of me as my living heart, my lungs, my lips and eyes. My love for my wife and daughter is well known to those around me, and yet it has happened that a woman in the camp—a woman of great beauty, admired by all of the men—has become attracted to me without my knowledge. This woman (I will call her Leila here) is not only beautiful but friendly, too, in an innocent way; a woman of smiles and pleasant words. She had made a difficult and dangerous journey to Australia from her homeland with her cousin, for her husband had been killed in her native land and she was without a man who could guard her and care for her and support her. I admire this woman for her bravery, and I pity her for her unhappy situation. Although she is friendly and always happy to make conversation, I can see in her eyes sometimes the wounds of widowhood. She is lonely.

She is unprotected. The husband she has lost she surely loved.

Today, I find this woman in tears in a quiet place within the camp, away from the eyes of others. I am driving the mule, on my way back from the mess, and I glimpse her some distance away, sheltering herself. I stop the mule and call to her, for even from a distance I can see her distress. She raises her hand in greeting, but the tears that shake her do not cease. So I leave the mule and walk to her, puzzled over what is troubling her—or what is troubling her today especially. I call to her.

'Leila, if you will excuse me I can't help noticing your tears. Some bad news, perhaps?'

Leila speaks fluent Dari after spending some of her early years in Afghanistan.

'Bad news?' she says. 'No, Najaf. You have caught me in a moment of weakness. But how strange that it should be you who has come to comfort me.'

'Why do you say that?'

'Can you not guess?'

Leila has been looking away from me a little, not into my eyes. This is normal in conversations between an Afghani man and a woman who is not his wife. Relations between Muslim men and women are often very formal or, I should say, follow certain rules that can make them look muffled or stiff or even evasive to a non-Muslim. Actually, Muslim men and women understand each other very well. Flirtation is out of the question, and yet we find ways to show our goodwill and our warmth of feeling. As I stand talking to Leila, she understands without me saying so that my heart is touched by her situation. It is not necessary for me to embrace her in order to show my concern. And there is something else I must explain. Without touching and without very much direct eye contact, Muslim women can let a man know a thousand things. A slight tilt of the head means one thing; a tiny gesture of the hand means another; the way in which a woman moves her veil a fraction of a centimetre means another thing still. A whole language of movements and small gestures takes the place of touching and of words. It is all very subtle. Somebody who has the time might write a dictionary of this language of signs.

But having said all this, I must now explain that on this day, Leila abandons this subtle language of which I have been speaking. She looks straight into my eyes in such a way that I am left embarrassed, for her gaze has let me know that her feeling for me goes far beyond friendliness.

'Leila,' I say to her, 'your unhappiness leads you down a path of trouble.'

She nods her head, but the pain remains in her eyes.

'You are a good person, Najaf. I have known it since first I met you. I have known it before I even greeted you for the first time. All of you Afghanis are good people. Should I feel ashamed to say that I would like to marry such a man as you?'

I am overcome with embarrassment now. I do not know where to look. But Leila knows where to look. She looks at my face.

'Leila, this cannot be.'

'No,' she says, and she looks away from me.

'Surely you know that I am married? Surely you know how much my wife and my child mean to me?'

'Yes, I know.'

'You force me to wound you. I hate to do so.'

'It is my fault. Do not distress yourself.'

She draws her veil a little closer around her face.

'A good man will come along,' I say, trying to find something that might console her. 'You are such a beautiful woman. A good man will find you and offer you his heart. God will see to it.'

She looks at me again, and this look is almost fierce, as if the words of consolation I am offering are like swords that pierce her flesh. I lift my hands helplessly. In all honesty, I am desperate to get away to some other place.

'God will see to it,' she says, but then she begins to shake and tears fall from her face like water running off a roof in the rain. Moaning sounds come from her; cries of pain. I have no idea of what to do. I cannot embrace her and hold her against my chest to comfort her. In the first place, as I've explained, that is just not the thing we do in my culture, unless perhaps the woman is very old. In the second place, Leila would surely take such an embrace as a strong sign of affection.

I can think of one thing only to console her. I have an apple in my pocket, one that I picked up in the mess, against regulations, to enjoy later. I take the apple from my pocket. It is a perfect apple, red and shining from the polishing I have given it. It has a sticker on it, a tiny label, as all the fruit we are served has attached, for some reason I cannot understand. It is necessary to peel off the label before eating the apple. Then it is necessary to find something to do with the label. I peel off the label and stick it on the back of my hand. Then I offer the apple to Leila, holding it before her.

'This is for you,' I say.

She looks at the apple, still heaving with sobs. Then she puts her hands to her face, and her cries and tears increase in a way that baffles me. But surely an apple is something!

I put the apple back in my pocket. It seems not to have met the welcome I'd thought it would.

'Leila,' I say, 'why not marry your cousin, the young man who came with you to this country? Surely he is the perfect man. He is young and strong. He is handsome. Why not marry your cousin?'

A few of the other refugees have noticed us. They slow down as they pass us, curious to hear what the trouble is all about. Leila has noticed these people and she attempts to gain control over her emotions.

'You had better leave me,' she says.

'But what of my suggestion? Your cousin?'

'First apples, now cousins,' Leila says, and with such anger. 'Have you anything else to offer? A palace, a prince?'

She turns away from me, heading for her dormitory.

'But there is your answer, Leila! Marry your cousin! Surely?'

She stops and turns her head.

'We are like brother and sister,' she says. 'Do you understand? Or have you another apple to offer me?'

She hurries away, almost running, and I am left shaking my head. Why should she be angry? Is it my fault if I love my wife and daughter? How have I become the person in the wrong?

I head back to the mule, still trying to puzzle out Leila's behaviour.

14

Land of Armies

ONE YEAR AFTER the rocket attack and one month after the miracle of the red pills, my leg was well mended and I was able to return to the rug factory. My boss was surprised to see me. The last he'd heard, I was crocheting socks on a street corner and seemed likely to be making my living in that way for the rest of my miserable life. But he was pleased as well as surprised, and I settled back into my education as a rugmaker. The great stone that had rested on my heart rolled away.

After a single hour back at my craft, I was more sure than ever that this was what I wanted to do forever—to make rugs, to learn more about the history of my craft, to develop my skill, and one day—a blessed day that would be—design rugs myself. It seemed to me that the sounds of the weaving room were welcoming me back; the movement of hands passing the treadle through the strands of yarn on the loom; the joking and bantering of the weavers; the occasional raised voice of the master—all of these sounds combined to make a music that caressed my ears. I thought to myself, 'See, Najaf, how the world is fashioned. A rocket crashes through your roof, your brother is killed, your mother is wounded, your leg is torn, but all that God asks of us is persistence.'

After a few months back in the factory, I was weaving simple quality rugs without assistance. After all, it does not take so long to learn to weave. Anyone can learn under the guidance of a master in half a year. But then come the more difficult skills—learning to repair rugs, to stretch rugs, to match colours, make colours, create a design that does justice to fine yarns. I was introduced to these more demanding skills gradually. It was during my initiation into the deeper mysteries of my craft that I began to understand how a world can exist within a single room. For when my concentration was at its greatest, it felt that the world lived in the yarns, in the colours and in the skills of rug-making. I don't know if it is strictly true to say so, but I like to believe that there is a moment in the life of each person when the eye of God ceases from its restless scanning of the plains and rivers and mountains and cities and rests its gaze just on you. And at such a moment, God says, 'Ah, that's Najaf, he has found the path I intended for him. I will watch him working for my own pleasure.'

My employment in life was settled, but the pleasure of God in my choice was not so great that He forgot other trials he intended for me, and for the whole of Afghanistan.

It was 1983 in the Western calendar when I returned to the rug factory. In my short lifetime, my country had been ruled by four presidents, and three of the four—Mohammad Daoud

Khan, Nur Mohammad Taraki and Hafizullah Amin—had been assassinated while in office. Afghanistan had been a one-party state for the whole of my life, and that one party was the communist party. I had no powerful feelings one way or the other about the communists. All that I hoped for was that they would leave me and my family alone. I had no powerful feelings about the mujahedin who opposed the communists, either; once again, I wanted them to leave me alone. And I would say that my feelings about the communists and the mujahedin were not any different from those of most Afghanis.

It was not that I took no interest in politics or in how my country was ruled; it was just that the communists and the mujahedin did not seem to me like people who had a grand plan for the salvation of Afghanistan. No, they seemed to me interested in ruling, and that was it. It was a power struggle in which the people in the struggle had forgotten everything about Afghanistan except their desire to rule it. Sometimes it seemed as if the two sides could fight until not a single building was left standing in the entire country, and the meadows and trees were burnt black, and the rivers full of bodies and rubble—just for the prize of ruling this wasteland. It was like two boxers fighting in the boxing ring, striking each other over and over until both were covered in bruises and blood. One of the boxers would finally fall down dead, but the other would be a cripple for the rest of his life. How could I, or how could anyone believe that these people were thinking of the good of the country?

Babrak Karmal was President when I returned to the rug factory. He wanted me to join his army and fight the mujahedin, even though I was barely into my teenage years. The mujahedin also wanted me to fight on their side. It was not just me that these two sides wanted, of course; they wanted every young Afghani male they could get their hands on. I had to spend half my life hiding from the recruitment officers of both sides. For neither side took any interest in the views of the young men and boys they were attempting to recruit.

The communists did not say, 'Are you a committed communist? Would you like to fight to spread communism all over Afghanistan?'

The mujahedin did not say, 'If you are an anti-communist, join us.' They did not care about all that. They only needed us to carry a gun and shoot people on the other side.

A few months before I returned to the rug factory, two officers of the army came upon me making socks on the street corner. I had to sit with my injured leg thrust straight out in front of me, because I could not bend it at the knee. It was obvious to everyone that I was in no state to join an army and fight. But the two officers swept such objections aside.

'Look at my leg,' I said to the more senior officer. 'I can barely walk.'

'So what?' he said. 'You can cook. We'll give you a stool and you can peel vegetables.'

'I can't sit on a stool,' I said.

'Sit on the floor, then.'

'I can't cook.'

'Everyone can cook. It's a mess hall, not a restaurant.'

'I'm too young,' I said.

'Who cares?'

The other officer said, 'Maybe he is too young. Look at him.'

The senior officer studied me suspiciously. He knelt down and took my chin in his hand and gazed at my face.

'No beard,' he said. 'How old are you?'

'Ten,' I lied, for I was thirteen, in truth. A boy of thirteen in Afghanistan is considered to be on the threshold of early manhood. And indeed, I had been expected to act more like an adult than a boy for a couple of years now. That was why I had expected Rosal Ali to listen to me when I gave him orders. Above eleven years old, a boy is an honorary man.

'Don't lie. How old are you?'

'Eleven. I mean I'll be eleven next week.'

'Eleven is good. We'll teach you how to boil rice.'

They went away and left me to myself, but I knew they would be back. They didn't believe that I was ten or eleven. They believed that I was just on the border of entry age into their army, which was around fifteen.

After that visit, I kept my eyes peeled as I sat making socks. I could see up and down the streets quite a way. If the mujahedin came back, I would wrap up all my socks in my kilim and disappear. And I wouldn't be alone in hiding. All over Mazar-e-Sharif, boys of my age and older were concealing themselves wherever they could to escape the mujahedin and the communists. If they found a boy, they always studied his face for the first signs of facial hair, as they had studied my face, or told him to roll up his trouser legs to see if the hair on his legs was growing darker. Sometimes you would see a boy sprinting down the street as if he was running in the Olympic Games, with recruitment officers chasing him. It was the national sport of Afghanistan, running away from the army. If the recruitment officers came to your house, you always had a hiding place prepared. The officers would come in and look around then ask the man who was the head of the house where such-and-such a person was. The head of the house would always say something like, 'Oh, you mean our Ali! No, we haven't seen him for weeks. We think he went to Kandahar to buy a camel.' It was not uncommon for the recruitment officers from the mujahedin to be followed closely by those of the communists, and so the same story would be told twice in a day.

It was worthwhile making a big effort to avoid being recruited into either army, because once you were in, you were dead. They did not want us in order to make us pilots of jet planes. They wanted us to stand and fight and kill other boys until finally one of the other boys killed us.

Even after I returned to the rug factory, I still had to be ready to run if the recruitment officers appeared in the neighbourhood. I could rely on news being sent ahead of the officers. A network like a telephone service had developed, and one person would pass the news on to another, and that person to a third person. One part of my brain was always on alert, ready to respond to signals, and not just the signal of a message in words. If I was walking down the street and heard the sound of running footsteps, I tensed and looked quickly about. Or if I heard the sound of a disturbance in the bazaar, raised voices, I prepared myself for a sprint to a hiding place. Even sounds coming from a great distance put me on edge—a dog suddenly barking, or the racket of birds rising into the air. I, and everyone in my position, maintained the sort of vigilance that we would have had to practise if we really *had* been in the army, and were listening for the sound of a Kalashnikov, or the whistle of a missile.

By the time of my early teenage years, war had become the main industry of Afghanistan—the main industry and the biggest employer, for the country kept not just one army but two. As I worked at the loom in the rug factory, I had to train myself not to think too far into the future. But it would happen at times that I would find myself deeply absorbed in my work and full of happiness at the prospect of learning more and more about my craft, and then I would suddenly realise that this future of learning and gaining greater and greater skill all depended on things that I couldn't control. I couldn't force the communists and the mujahedin to make peace; I couldn't force the Russians to go home and look after their own business in Russia. I couldn't say to the recruitment officers, 'What you are doing can never return this land to happiness, find some other job for yourselves.' And so I would wonder, just for a few moments at a time, if there was another future for me in another country. But even those few moments of thinking were too much for my heart. I may as well have been thinking of turning myself into a fish and living in the ocean. It could not be. Not ever.

15

The Other Side of the Fence

IN CANBERRA, IN THE place where visas are made, some people remain awake all night. The man who puts his special stamp on a piece of paper—that man is at his desk from sunrise to sunrise. For visas sometimes arrive here in Main Camp very late at night, and when that happens an officer will find a man sound asleep and say to him, 'Good news for you, my friend. We want you to stay.'

I am myself sound asleep this night in the dormitory dreaming of I don't know what—maybe of watermelons, maybe of my wife, maybe of a Holden car with automatic gears that I am steering down the streets of Australia. Whatever my dream is, a great bear has walked into it and thrown himself on me, for I am being shaken roughly by the shoulders. I mutter in Dari, 'In the name of God!' and against my will, force myself awake. What I see first is the face of my friend, Nemat. He is sitting on the side of his bed, close to mine. He is smiling all over his shining face as if he had just discovered a gold mine. It looks to me as if he has lost his wits. A security officer is standing by the side of my bed and he, too, is smiling.

'What has happened?' I ask, for I don't really trust the smiles of the two men. For me, the middle of the night is not a good time. I have only memories of disaster at such times.

'Be glad, brother,' says Nemat. 'The visas have come.'

'The visas have come?'

'Yes, brother. A visa for you and a visa for me.'

I leap from my bed and find myself dancing with Nemat. The security officer is trying to get our attention but I have to let out some of my joy or else I will fall on the floor and begin weeping for joy.

'It is my pleasure to inform you that the Commonwealth of Australia, through the agency of...'

I interrupt the officer.

'Is it true? Is it true about the visas?'

'Yeah, it's true,' says the officer, and begins again to read something from a piece of paper.

'It is my pleasure to inform you that the Commonwealth of Australia, through the agency of the Department of...'

I don't hear any more. I have resumed my dance with Nemat. As we dance, Nemat shouts at me, 'I told you! I told you! I had a dream that this would be our fate!'

Other people have been woken from their sleep. In the light of the torch, I can see the white teeth of people smiling at us, and smiling for us. Everyone loves to hear that visas have come because it means that there is hope. Well, almost everyone. Someone is calling out in Dari, asking us if we are human beings or owls, who shriek in the night.

We go together to the shower block, where we can talk without disturbing anyone. We are like little children who have been promised sweets in the morning and who cannot sleep for joy.

'But how can it be that such news comes in the night?' says Nemat. 'It is three o'clock!'

'Who knows?' I say. 'Is there a bad time for good news? Do you wish you were still asleep?'

'Now life can begin, just as my dream said it would.'

'Nemat, brother, you and I are the happiest people in the world. Nowhere is anyone happier than us. This place here, this poor shower block is the happiest place in the world. Imagine that!'

We speak of our plans. We try not to let our joy overcome us, but it is hard work. Adults have given up the right to leap and laugh like children, to put their hands to their face and feel wet tears running through their fingers, and yet that was what we wanted to do. But finally we feel that it is undignified to hold each other by the shoulders and blubber with happiness, and we regain control of ourselves and walk back to the dormitory.

The security officer who had brought us the wonderful news is waiting for us.

Something is the matter with his face. His smile has disappeared, and he now looks as if he will never smile again in this life. My heart rolls over in my chest and a sick feeling spreads all through me. Nemat beside me is as still as a stone statue.

'A mistake,' says the security officer.

'What?'

'A mistake. I am sorry, very, very sorry. The visas are not for you.'

157

'Not for us?'

'No. I apologise.'

I can't make my brain work. I understand the English word, 'mistake', but my brain won't let me believe it.

'No visas for us?'

'No.'

'But you said!' I burst out, speaking my own language in my despair. 'How could there be a mistake? You said the visas have come!'

Nemat puts his hand on my shoulder. He is as broken-hearted as me, but maybe his life has taught him that wonderful things can be snatched away. Maybe he didn't believe it, deep, deep down. But I believed it.

The security officer looks down at his feet and shakes his head. He lifts his hands in resignation. I can see how painful it is for him to bring us this news, but that doesn't make me feel sorry for him. Who feels sorry for the poor man who brings bad news? In some countries, I have heard, such a man is taken away and shot.

We return to our beds. I try to sleep, but sleep won't come. I say to myself, over and over, 'No tears, Najaf!'

In the morning, I force myself to do all the things I normally do. I take the mule to the depot and stack it with stores for the mess. I smile when people greet me. I wave to the guards whose names I know. I bless God at the right time. I eat my breakfast. But my heart is like an empty cave where darkness lasts all through the day and water drips from the roof. This 'mistake' in the night has reminded me that life for an adult—and indeed, even for a child—is mostly about learning to overcome disappointment. We have many more disappointments than days of wonderful news because we are human beings and we are given a hoping heart by God. If God did not give us the power to hope, we would not have lasted long on His earth. So we must learn to keep standing straight when disappointment falls onto our shoulders. I say to myself, 'Najaf, there is joy for you in the life you live, but this was the night, and when has night ever done you a favour? Wait for the day. If good news comes, it will come in the light of day.' These words I speak to myself do not make my heart any lighter, but what can I do? Just as I could not give myself the freedom to shriek with laughter and clap my hands when I stood with Nemat in the shower block, so now I cannot give myself the freedom to sink down to my knees and weep. Do I need to say this? You, who hold this book in your hands and read my words on the page—like me, you have felt this way in your heart, surely that is true? You have stopped in the work you must do and heaved a sigh from the deepest part of yourself. You have whispered when no one else can hear, 'I can't go on,' and yet you have placed one foot before another and made yourself continue the journey. This is what people do. They place one foot in front of the other and go on with the journey, like the old camel I spoke of before who sees the mountain before him and saves his laments for later.

Weeks pass in this way. Others in the camp console me. 'Surely the Australians will reward you for your hard work, brother. Be brave.'

I smile, as I must, and reply, 'It is in the hands of God. He sees all the way to Australia.' Do I believe it? Yes. I believe it is in the hands of God. Oh, but so many times I thought that I understood what God intended for me, so many times I thought I could see into His heart. But it's not possible. And just as well.

Let me accept the fate that has been fashioned for me. Of all the mistakes I make in my life, let me not add arguing with God to the list.

I pause in my duties each day to gather up my courage; sometimes more than once, sometimes more than twice. I look out through the fence to the land of Australia all around me. The daydreams in my head form pictures on the barren soil of the desert. The words of songs come to my lips; songs of grief. But I never sing more than a line or two.

✳ ✳ ✳

I am asleep in my bed in the dormitory, and my sleep is deep. Again, I cannot say what I am dreaming about, but I dream all the time so something must be happening in my head. And again the big bear intrudes into my dream and takes hold of me and shakes me with his strong arms.

'Najaf! Wake up! Wake up, kid!'

It is the security officer—the same one who woke me weeks earlier. I glimpse his face only for a second, at the same time noticing the light of morning that shows behind the curtains on the windows.

'Go!' I say, and I pull my blanket over my head. I want my sleep back. Whatever my dreams were, I want to return to them.

'Wake up! Come on, kid. Wake yourself up!'

He pulls the blanket away from my face. His leans down close to me. He is smiling, the same smile I saw on his face when he came with good news that was not good news.

'No!' I say to him. What I mean by that, I don't have all

the English words for. I mean that I am not ready for another mistake. I mean that I have used up all the strength I have recovering from the last mistake. I mean that I have made what peace I can with Australia, and Australians, and with the entire world of mistakes, and with security officers, and interviewers, and with the mysterious man in the city of Canberra who is the keeper of the special stamp. I mean that I desire nothing more in the world now than another hour of sleep.

The security officer reaches down and takes hold of my hand. He grips it firmly, as if to show his confidence and to give some of that confidence to me. He looks at my face without saying anything. He is not smiling now. His expression is serious, but not severe.

'Najaf, this time it's true. Your visa has come.'

I shake my head. 'No,' I tell him.

'Your visa has come. No mistakes, I promise you.'

'My visa?'

'Yes. Your visa. Many visas. They came this morning.'

'It's true?'

'I promise.'

I lift myself up from the bed and rest my weight on my elbow.

'Is it morning?' I ask.

'Yep.' The security officer looks at his watch. 'A bit after six.'

I nod my head.

'I'll leave you to it,' the security officer says, and he departs.

I sit on the side of my bed, trying to make my mind up. Will I believe him? Will I wait for an hour? An hour is enough time for the Australians to discover that another mistake has been made.

161

And yet the security officer was certain. He is not a cruel man. He would not torment me.

I decide to wait. I dress myself, go to the shower block, wash my face, brush my teeth. I do everything slowly, carefully. Whenever I see another Afghani who is speaking of his joy, speaking of the visas that have come, I nod and smile, but I do not necessarily believe him. For all I know, I am still asleep. And yet, in my heart I know I am awake.

On the way back from the shower block, I stop and stand still with my towel over my shoulder. I look out through the fence to the dry land around me, and to the sky. I can see a part of the road that comes to Woomera from the world. Away to the east, the sun is standing just above the horizon with a haze around it. A bird, the name of which I do not know, swoops over the fence and seems about to find a place for itself on the gutter of the roof nearby, but then it changes its mind and heads away back into the desert.

All at once, I know that it is true. My visa has come. It is nothing to do with the security officer and nothing to do with the other Afghanis who believe him. It is just to do with my heart. I am not full of joy, but a much slower type of happiness is growing inside me. The other side of the fence—that is my home. It is strange, but I am certain that this moment was waiting for me to reach it for years and years.

16

Strawberries

WAR HAD ALWAYS been the background to my life (and sometimes much more than background) and it surely helped to form the way I thought about things. In a way, war had become normal in Afghanistan; it was peace that was strange. At the same time, war never truly seemed normal to me. It was as if I had an idea in my mind of what peace was like; an idea that must have been put there by my mother and father, by Gorg Ali—people who had known peace in their lifetimes. I don't mean to say that every day of my life was filled with explosions; not at all. In Shar Shar and in Mazar-e-Sharif, the war would disappear for days and weeks and months. Fighting is difficult in winter, for example, and the guns go quiet for a time. But even when the fighting died down, everybody knew that it was just the snow and the cold and the rain that was the cause. When the fighting started again, it was unpredictable.

Alliances would change, and all at once one warlord would be fighting alongside another warlord who used to be his enemy. Or one side would launch an attack in a part of the country where things had been quiet. You never knew what was going to happen, but you knew with certainty that peace would not suddenly take the place of war.

But people cannot live like that. They cannot wake up each day and think, 'Probably, I will be blown up today.' The people of Afghanistan lived as if a normal life was still possible. They made plans for the future. They married. They had children. They built houses. And as for me, I studied my craft as a rugmaker as if I would be weaving at a loom until I was old and grey.

When I returned home from the rug factory each evening, my mother and my brother and my sister and my in-laws greeted me according to the proof I had given of my reliability. As a boy of 13, they thought of me as an honorary man, yes, but as a man who was still capable of suddenly getting it into his head to give up rug-making and take up something that was more exciting. But after a year back at the loom, and then two years, they began to take me more seriously. What they saw was a boy who seemed to accept that life was all to do with hard work, and they approved. What they didn't see was the joy I took in my work, the excitement I felt when I learnt something new, such as dyeing and stretching and mending a rug so that the repair was a perfect match in colour and texture. I didn't speak to them very much about my pleasure in learning my craft. All of the members of my family had work of their own and worries of their own. What they wanted to hear and see was a boy who was not going to cause them the sort of trouble that my brother

Rosal Ali had caused. Such is the way of things in an Afghani family. A child or a teenager is not treated as if he were a project; no, a boy of my age is given a slap around the ears if he makes trouble, and if he does not, then maybe he'll be rewarded with a few brief words of praise once or twice a year. It's enough.

And so I settled into the rhythm of adulthood when I was no more than 15. It was a rhythm with a difference, though; I had to make sure that I regularly dodged around corners and sprinted up alleyways to avoid the recruiters of the mujahedin and the communists. It became part of normal life: rise in the morning, wash my face, clean my teeth, eat the breakfast that was prepared by my mother, honour God, take my lunch in my hand and walk to work, meet a young man on the way running in the opposite direction as if the devil was chasing him with a pitchfork, take to my heels myself, find one of a dozen little niches where I could hide myself for a half hour, pop my head out when all seemed safe, continue my journey to the rug factory, apologise to my boss for being late, take a deep breath and let it out with a low whistle to show that I'd been running and had exhausted my lungs. And then, of course, settle down on a folded rug before my loom, cross my legs and return to the weaving at the point I had left it the previous afternoon.

Living in this way, time rolls along. You age a little, you look at things in a different way. Marriage seems a world away, then one day, after your sixteenth birthday, you begin to think—and that is what happened to me. Instead of just having thoughts that came into my head, I *made* thoughts come into my head. I thought about marriage. It would be years before I could really make the first steps toward marriage, but I was free at least to imagine the sort of woman I could settle down with. Even at 16,

I didn't contemplate a woman of ravishing beauty and a smile that would make me wobble at the knees. I was too serious for that. But I must explain to you that I was not serious in the way that scholars are, like Talibs, who sit over the Koran all day and never have a thought about anything other than their studies. No, when I say I was 'serious', I mean that I was serious about life. I did not think that life was a grand adventure, nor did I think it was a mere dream, and nor did I think it was just a journey on the way to a happier life in paradise. I thought life was work and building and finding a path to a small share of the prosperity of the earth and raising children I would love and who would love me. It was not a huge dream, but a modest one, for it seemed to me that in the plans of God, I had been given a modest part to play.

But there is something else that made me think about marriage in such a serious way when I was still so young, and that has to do with the culture of the Afghanis, and of Muslims. In the West, getting married is a practical step in life, yes, but love of a very strange sort is such a big part of it. It is 'strawberry' love. The girlfriend and then the wife of the man in the West is like a huge basket of strawberries, and these are miraculous strawberries for no matter how many you eat, the basket remains full. This man has never seen such beautiful strawberries, red and plump and shining. He thinks, 'To have these strawberries every day for the whole of my life—this is paradise, for I love strawberries.' But who can eat strawberries every day without growing tired of them? And so the man looks about for a fruit of another sort, and of course he finds a whole bazaar full of baskets: raspberries, figs, plums, and all of them seem much more appealing than strawberries. This sort of love can be used up, and once it is used up, what remains? Distaste, boredom. In Afghanistan, a man looks for what will nourish him for the whole of his life, and what could nourish him more than bread? Who thinks of bread as a food you devour until you are tired of it? Bread is on the table every day, and every day it sustains you. And so, for me, for most men of Afghanistan, a wife is the bread of our life. In every land, bread is honoured and thanks given to God for its appearance on the table.

I thought, too, of children, for I was fashioning in my head the life I desired and what life can satisfy us unless there are children to love? A child is one of God's ways of showing his love for you, and in loving the child, you show your love for God.

All of these thoughts I carried with me each day, and I worked with them in my mind just as I worked with the yarn on the loom. I was weaving my life, making a pattern that pleased me, drawing the knots tight, searching for the best quality wools, the most lasting dyes. And it was this double weaving, in my mind and on the loom, that kept my spirits high when the mujahedin chased me and the communists chased me and the war went on and on and the jets roared across the blue skies.

* * *

In the year 1986 in the Western calendar, when I was 15 years old, Dr Mohammad Najibullah was elected President of Afghanistan, taking the place of Babrak Karmal. Najibullah had been the head of the secret police and what crimes he had on his hands would be painful to even imagine. Certainly there was no rejoicing in my family. The fighting between the communists and the mujahedin became ever more fierce, and more and more young men disappeared from the streets of Mazar-e-Sharif. We knew that in many parts of Afghanistan, people were packing up all they owned and heading east to find safety in Pakistan. The war found ways to surprise us even as we thought that we would never be surprised by anything that the government forces or the mujahedin did. Did we believe that the communists and the mujahedin had some strategy to triumph and rid the land of battlefields and so bring peace to Afghanistan? Even when we despaired, did we not in some part of our hearts hope that something would happen to make peace possible, even if only for a year or two? If we hoped in that way, it was a foolish hope. Neither side had any plan except to fight until the death. By fighting until the death, they meant the death of everyone, if necessary.

The Russians began to leave Afghanistan in 1988. In eight years, they had accomplished nothing at all, except to keep the communist government in power. Najibullah changed the name of his party from communist to Watan, which means 'homeland'. He had to make this change. The Russians had so much trouble back in their own Watan that they couldn't support Najibullah with money and guns and aeroplanes any longer. Najibullah wanted us all to believe that the war was all about our homeland, and about democracy; it was not about communism at all.

As I write this, it might sound to my readers as if I knew what was going on and could follow the changes just by looking out from the roof of my house—looking out to see trucks full of Russians heading north, for example. But it was not like that. In a war such as the war in Afghanistan you know very little. News came to us in Mazar-e-Sharif in the newspapers or from the television or from gossip, but such news doesn't make anything clear, since it is mostly propaganda. All you know is the habits of the sides. You know that the government forces will call in air strikes and if need be, blow up many innocent people, and that the mujahedin will swarm into a village and find those who have supported the government forces and shoot them. You know the sort of language that the two sides use; the government side always talking about the welfare of the people and the mujahedin talking about the will of God. You know when one side has had a victory because the leaders of the victorious side will start to talk as if the end of the war is only a few days away. You know when one side has suffered a defeat because the leaders of the defeated side will talk about their determination to fight for victory even if it takes 1000 years. That is all you know: habits.

I became an adult with war raging all over Afghanistan. In 1992, the mujahedin swarmed into Kabul and claimed the capital for its own. But the mujahedin was never really a united force; it was made up of dozens of smaller forces and the only thing that held them together was hatred of the communists. Ahmad Shah Massoud was the first of the mujahedin leaders to enter Kabul, but another leader, Gulbuddin Hekmatyar, who headed the Hizb-i-Islami force of the mujahedin moved into Kabul soon after and the two forces fought each other as bitterly as they had fought the Russians and the government troops. In 1992, my country had no fewer than three presidents: Najibullah, then Sibghatullah Mujadidi, then Burhanuddin Rabbani. The Uzbeks were also involved in running Afghanistan for a short time, because Rabbani was supported by an Uzbeki warlord, General Abdul Rashid Dostum.

Through all this chaos, my family lived as best it could. For my part, I took my interest in marriage a step further, at age 21, and declared my interest in a woman who was the friend of a friend. This woman had already declared her interest in me. Whenever I turned around, she was there. If I wanted a cup of tea at my friend's place, she had a cup in my hand before I had even finished speaking. She liked me; she liked me very, very much, and in my country of Afghanistan, it is a bad policy for a woman to show that she likes a man so much. I told my mother about my desire to marry this woman, as custom demanded, since all such arrangements are made by the mother; her approval is the start of any engagement, and her disapproval is the end of it. And my mother disapproved without stopping to draw breath after her gasp of astonishment.

'No,' she said.

'No? Why do you say no?'

'I say no because I say no. No.'

'A reason, at least!'

My mother waved her hand in my direction while looking away in another direction, as if to dismiss my request as too foolish to even pay attention to. But then she seemed to think again, perhaps wishing to educate me, and she came and sat down and looked me in the eye.

'She runs after you,' she said.

'I don't deny it, but is that such a bad thing?'

'Listen to me, Najaf. You are a child and you know nothing. A woman who runs after you today may run after another man tomorrow. You can't trust such women. No, not ever.'

She left me thinking about what she'd said. It was true that I had no great experience of women. How could I? In my culture, we do not study women, we do not go out on dates, we do not go to bed with each other before marriage. I had no opportunity to learn. After listening to my mother, I had to ask myself if there were secret things about women that only other women could see. Perhaps there were many secret things, not visible to the eyes of men. People have such mysterious knowledge, not only about women, but about other living creatures, such as horses and camels. There are men who can look at a horse or a camel and tell you about its whole life—where it was bred, where it was raised, if it has had any illnesses, how reliable it is, how fast it can run, if it has a sweet temper or a bad temper. But now it sounds as if I am comparing women with horses and camels, and that is not what I mean. What do I mean? I have no idea.

After my mother's lesson to me about women who run after a man, I put all thoughts of marriage out of my mind for a time. I thought only about rug-making and avoiding both sides in the new war of mujahedin against mujahedin. And I thought of something else, too; I thought of the Taliban. These people, the Taliban, were spoken of more and more in the newspapers and on the streets. They were of the mujahedin, but different from any mujahedin of the past. At first, I thought of these new warriors that I had yet to see in a scornful way. 'Talib' means 'student', but students in Afghanistan were not supposed to look up from their studies for even a minute. These students wandered all over the country with guns and grenade-launchers. I did not accept them as genuine students.

Before long, these men who called themselves Taliban had succeeded in making people set aside everything that they thought they knew about the mujahedin. It became obvious that these new warriors were fanatics, without any concern for anything other than fighting and worship. In areas where they had won victories over the other mujahedin forces, they made ordinary people afraid to leave their houses. They published a code that made all sorts of things illegal that had once been accepted as a normal part of life. Music was gone, singing was gone, instruments that made music were gone, dancing was gone, laughter was gone, books were gone except for the holy book.

I was then, and I remain, a man of religion. I honour God. I know of no other way for a man to live his life. Those who honour other gods than mine—peace to them, forever. Those who honour no God at all—peace to them, too. I would never raise a sword, never even raise a feather cushion against another man because of his religion, or because of his lack of religion. I cannot live in a comfortable way beside men who wish to cut the throats of those they find fault with in the way they worship. I cannot live comfortably beside the Taliban. From the time I first heard of them, I thought, 'Najaf, a bad wind will carry these men to your doorstep. Have courage!'

I think I must say more about the Taliban, for people in the West think of these people as a scourge that came out of nowhere. But the truth is that they came out of India, in the days when the British ruled that country. The Muslims of India feared that the British would destroy their religious culture, so they set up schools, very strict schools, to educate Muslims in Muslim culture. They were known as Deobandi schools—that was the name of the movement that was trying to save Islamic traditions under British rule. Once the British left India and the Muslim nation of Pakistan was created, the Deobandi kept on with their work, mostly amongst very poor people. And that was the problem, for the Deobandi schools were run by mullahs who were themselves very poorly educated; they only knew how to read the Holy Book in a very simple way. But the Holy Book is not a simple book. You need brains to understand what is being said, otherwise you are missing everything. The Deobandi mullahs didn't care if they were missing everything; they wanted a simple set of rules, very harsh ones, to teach the poor, for how could these uneducated people be expected to follow a complicated story? Educated Muslims in Pakistan thought of these Deobandi mullahs and their students as primitive people and laughed at them, but in a poor country, if you laugh at the poor you end up laughing at a great many people.

In the Muslim world, there are not many rich nations, but for many years now there has been at least one very rich nation, and that is Saudi Arabia. The Saudis are Sunnis, mostly, and the Pakistanis and Afghanis are also mostly Sunni. The Saudis gave money to the Deobandis, and they gave them instructions too: they wanted the money to be used for the teaching of the Wahhabi tradition in the Deobandi schools. Wahhabi is the most fundamentalist form of Islam. So the teaching of the Deobandi mullahs was made even stricter by the Wahhabi philosophy. When the Russians came to my country in 1980, the war created millions of refugees. And the mujahedin civil war that followed when the Russians pulled out nine years later made millions more people homeless. Where could these people go to escape the fighting? They were the poorest people in Afghanistan. They could not jump on an aeroplane and fly to a friendly country. No, they packed up what they owned— very little—and carried these few possessions eastwards into the border provinces of Pakistan. Whole cities of Afghani refugees grew up in Pakistan. These people had no money, no employment. They brought something with them apart from their pots and pans and rugs and tools—they brought a hatred of the corruption and lies of the warlords and provincial governors and politicians who had played their part in driving them into exile. Old people know how to despair, but young men know how to hate. They have years of life left to them. If they swear an oath of revenge, they mean what they are saying. The Deobandi mullahs took the young people into their schools and made their hatred and disgust stronger than ever. These young people, these scholars, became the Taliban, and when they were old enough, they left the Deobandi schools, swore a vow and made the journey westwards back into Afghanistan with Kalashnikovs in their hands.

In centuries past, Afghanis could use swords as if they had witchcraft in their hands but in modern fighting, the sword is of little use. Now, every young Afghani who has served in the army or in the mujahedin is a genius with firearms, with grenade-launchers, with arms of any sort. Put an assault rifle into the hands of a young mujahedin and in two minutes he will know how to strip it and reassemble it and in five minutes he will be able to use it as if he were raised with it in his hands from infancy. On top of this genius with firearms, Afghanis of the mujahedin fight like no other people on earth, as I have already said. No one must think that I am boasting about the courage of my countrymen when I say that they cannot be defeated in guerrilla combat. Americans have a genius for business and they work at making their fortunes year after year, the Japanese can make cars like no one else and will never stop making cars, the French produce the best wine in the world (so it is said) and in a hundred years they will still be making the best wine. Afghanis are the best in the world at close-range fighting, and because they are the best, they keep doing it. But even the mujahedin, as skilled as they were at fighting, had never come across anyone like the Taliban before.

No matter how great a fighter you are, the day comes when you wake up in the morning and see the snow on the ground and feel the cold air on your face, and think, 'No fighting today. Today I sleep.' And so you take the day off. Or maybe there is a wedding feast to attend, and so you think, 'This is an important wedding, the wedding of my cousin, I'll take a week off.' Or it could happen that the warlord you fight for has made a deal with the warlord you were fighting against, and so you say, 'This may not last for long, but while it does, I'll enjoy a holiday.' And you take a month off. But the Taliban did not take a month off, and not even a week off, and not even a day off. They woke from sleep with their guns in their hands and were ready to fight within ten seconds. They could not be bribed. They did not attend weddings, even if the wedding was important. They lived to fight and they had no doubts at all about what they were doing. The mullahs had taught them that God had no time for doubts.

But you do not want to live in a country ruled by people who never have any doubts. To have doubts is human. A horse has no doubts, a grasshopper has no doubts, an ant has no doubts. But a human being stops to think sometimes, and when he thinks, he hears a voice asking quietly, 'Are you certain that you are right? You must be certain before you pull that trigger. You must be certain before you put your knife to that man's throat.' Would God have given us the power to question if he wanted us to behave like horses and grasshoppers and ants? I am sure

God takes pleasure in all the creatures of the world, but I am also sure that his greatest pleasure is a human being who puts his knife away because he is not sure, because a doubt has come into his mind.

The ill wind I had feared that carried the Taliban to every corner of my country came to my corner later than to some others. In 1996, Mazar-e-Sharif was guarded by the United Front, a coalition of Northern League forces that included the Hazara militia. The great Hazara leader, Abdul Ali Mazari, had taken a stand against the Taliban, but not because he was Shi'a and the Taliban were mostly Sunni. He stood against them because he saw in the Taliban what he might have become if his heart had not been great. He was a man of strict religious practices, as the Talibs were. He was no friend of foreign invaders, just like the Talibs. He had no hunger for riches and could not be purchased, which was what everyone said of the Taliban. But he was a man who could stand in wonder and gaze at the beauty of things, and no Talib could do that.

In 1995, the Taliban and Mazari's forces were both independently fighting the Soviet-backed government troops in Kabul. The Taliban called Abdul Ali in for peace talks, and at those talks they killed him. They said he reached for his gun, which would be a strange thing to do at peace talks. They went to his house after they'd killed him and searched for the gold and dollars they thought he was hoarding. But his house was very plain, and there was no money to be found. The murder of Abdul Ali Mazari made every Hazara in Afghanistan an enemy of the Taliban.

And so later, when the Taliban came to take Mazar-e-Sharif, the Hazara fought them with all of their might, and defeated them. Two thousand five hundred Taliban soldiers were killed. It was the first defeat the Taliban had ever suffered.

Everyone in Mazar-e-Sharif knew that the Talibs would probably return one day. They held more than 80 per cent of the country but 80 per cent would not be enough for them. They wanted international recognition but wouldn't get that until they held power all over Afghanistan, and that meant taking Mazar-e-Sharif. The people of Mazar-e-Sharif did not make plans for an evacuation, or anything of that sort. I'm sure that everyone thought as I did: when they come, we will deal with it. Meanwhile, we acted as if the day when the Taliban would return was a long way off.

* * *

By 1997 I was well prepared for marriage and for the life I would lead as a married man. My work as a weaver in the rug factory meant that I could offer security to my wife and to the children we would have together. All of my friends and relatives knew this. I had become what would be called an eligible bachelor in the West. And so my friends and relatives, without saying anything to me, began to look about for a woman who would suit me. When I say 'suit me' I mean only that they were looking for an unmarried Hazara woman of child-bearing age. It is not necessary in Afghanistan, as it is in the West, to search for a wife who shares your interests and thinks in the same way as you. All Afghani women know that marriage means homemaking and children. All Afghani men know that marriage means working to keep bread on the table and a sheltering roof over his wife's head. It is not complicated.

I wanted to be married, with all my heart. I was 27 years old, well into adulthood. Once you are an adult, you can never again be a boy, and you wish it to be understood that the things of boyhood are in your past. In truth, most of the things I did when I was a boy were good things, happy things, but even if I'd wanted to hold onto them, a great force was pushing me from behind into the next stage of my life. I think this is true, all over the world. Perhaps we want to cry out, 'But wait! I wish for a few more years of playing with my friends, a few more years when I can be silly without people thinking that I am a fool!' Wish for that if you like, but the great force pushing you doesn't listen. It didn't listen when you were a child, with no responsibilities and with people to carry you in their arms when your legs were tired. You became a boy and had to use your own legs. Nor will it listen when you are a man of 60 and see the beginning of old age a little further up the road you tread. God expects that we will honour each stage of the life He has planned for us. He does not want adults who think they are still boys. It is cruel, in a way, but necessary.

One evening after the defeat of the Taliban at the gates of Mazar-e-Sharif, my friend Iajaz asked me to come to his house for dinner. This was not unusual. To sit and eat and drink tea with friends is one of the great pleasures of life for an Afghani. It was only when we were chatting that I realised that Iajaz had put me on display. His mother was quietly and courteously sizing me up. After a certain time had passed, Iajaz said, 'Did I ever mention to you, Najaf, soon my sister will be 27?' He had not even mentioned that he had a sister, much less one who would soon be 27.

'No, brother, you hadn't said anything to me about that.'

'How strange! But yes, indeed. She will be 27.'

'Is that true?'

'Oh, yes. Surely. Twenty-seven.'

'I see.'

We sat sipping our tea, without any further mention of my proposal of marriage. For that was what I had done in saying, 'I see'; I had proposed. I hadn't seen Iajaz's sister who was soon to turn 27, but the fact that she existed, and was of that age, and came from a good family meant that I could only decline if I was prepared to insult Iajaz, Iajaz's mother, the whole of Iajaz's family, and the memory of his ancestors, going back to the beginning of time. Such a thought never entered my head.

'More tea, Najaf?'

'Yes, brother. Of course.'

'Twenty-seven, Hakima will be, as I said.'

'That is how I heard you. Twenty-seven. Good health to her, and God's blessing.'

'Our thanks. Her health is excellent, as a matter of fact.'

'I see.'

'She enjoys the health of all the females in our family, if I may say so.'

'God has blessed you.'

'That is the truth. God has blessed us. Ah but it seems only yesterday that my sister was a child! And now she's almost 27. Time passes and suddenly, we are amazed!'

'Indeed! Time passes and suddenly, we are amazed!'

'Twenty-seven! Astonishing! We are proud of her.'

'I see.'

When I returned home that night, I told my mother that Iajaz had a sister. My mother said, 'Hmm.' Years had passed since my first, unsuccessful attempt to get myself married, but I was still concerned that my mother might have that secret knowledge I spoke about, and that she would scold me. But no, she seemed calm.

'Mother, visit Iajaz's family. Give me your judgement about the sister.'

My mother shrugged, opened her hands and closed them again.

'Son, it is your life and your choice. God will guide you.'

My choice? My mother was letting me believe that it was my choice if I married Hakima? There was no way in the world it would be left to my choice unless my mother already knew of Iajaz's sister and approved. By saying to me that it was my choice, my mother was really saying, 'I am prepared to let you believe that it is your choice.'

So I was engaged. It felt good. I said to my mother, 'She may not be beautiful.'

My mother shrugged again. I'm sure she could see that I was trying to prove to her that I was not swept away by looks and smiles.

'Your choice,' she said.

I was permitted, by custom, to meet with Hakima and talk with her before the wedding ceremony, but only in a very formal way. There was no flirting, for example, and in any case, I was very shy. I told Hakima that I was very pleased that she had accepted my offer of marriage, and promised to be a hard-working husband. I made a few comments about the weather, too. For her part, Hakima listened quietly and closely to my awkward words, nodding and agreeing whenever it was appropriate. Anybody watching us would have thought we were finding these meetings difficult, but the truth was that we were very happy. Hakima's eyes were bright and shining, and the blush that covered my face was really a blush of pleasure. I must explain to my readers that my shyness was not unusual. All unmarried Afghani men are shy when it comes to women.

My wedding was a city wedding, not a country wedding. People came in cars. In the country, guests arrive from near and far on horseback, in carriages, sometimes by camel. I have spoken of the rituals of an Afghani wedding, but my wedding was a simple ceremony and not every ritual was observed. We were not wealthy, after all. But from the first light of morning until I closed my eyes late at night, my heart was full. How many weddings had I attended? A hundred? But this one was mine—my wedding to Hakima. I had given my good wishes to so many grooms, I had raised a glass to so many brides, I had sat and listened to the musicians and admired them, I had piled my plate with food and piled it again, I had clapped with the other guests when the groom and bride departed, shouting blessings at the top of my voice—but on this day, my friends came to embrace me and kiss my cheeks. I thought of all the other members of my family who had felt a full heart on their wedding day, and I thought of my father who had died when I was young. I thought of my grandparents, and I imagined a long, long line of my ancestors stretching for a great distance, all of them married in just this way, except for the honking of car horns. The happiness I felt was of a different sort from any I had known before. For it is true, do you agree, that happiness is not all of the one sort? If you win a lottery, of course you feel happy. If you manage to avoid being forced into the army, that is happiness, or relief, at least. If you eat a fine meal, or see the smile on the face of your father when you have pleased him in some way, or share tea with your friends—all of these things will make you happy. And I had known great happiness of a special sort when I sat at the loom and saw the patterns of the weaving take shape and grow. But on my wedding day, the happiness I felt was new to me. It made me feel that our lives are important, however easily they can be snatched from us by a rocket exploding on the roof or a tiny germ that gets into our blood. I thought, many terrible things are true, but this is just as true: a fine wife such as Hakima, the smiling faces of my family and friends, the music of dara, tula, rubab and tambor filling the air, the blessing of God. At one time on that day, it happened that I was standing by myself for a short time gazing at the guests. Tears came into my eyes and I put my hand to my heart. 'Remember always what God can provide,' I said, speaking only to myself, and then I plunged back into the crowd.

It was necessary for me to recall that lesson very soon after—necessary to remember that life is more and better than the dread it can cause you. The Taliban returned, as we knew they would, and with them they brought all the terrors of Hell.

17

The Miracle of the Wire Brush

TASMANIA IS A LAND of green hills and rivers. It is said to resemble England. But tall trees grow in Tasmania, taller than any tree in England, and creatures with sharp teeth known as devils roam the forests, together with a strange type of tiger. Very little industry, many farms, many apples. Tasmania is where I asked to be sent when I left Woomera. I had heard about it from an education officer at Main Camp. My only skills were guarding sheep and the weaving and repair of Afghan traditional rugs. Weaving rugs seemed out of the question, but guarding sheep was a possibility. They had sheep in Tasmania.

But I have not been sent to Tasmania. I have been sent to Dandenong in the state of Victoria, a big city full of industries to the east of Melbourne. After waiting so long, I am here so suddenly. There are no sheep in Dandenong and no Afghan traditional rugs, either. But there are other Afghans, and Iraqis, some Iranians, a few Kurds. A house has been found for me in Dandenong where I live with three other Afghanis.

When the very big problems you face are finally fixed, you become aware that those big problems hid from your view one hundred smaller problems. I needed a visa and that, and worrying about Hakima and Maria, took up all the worry and concern I had to spare. The visa was given to me, and now I have to worry about a job, a place to live where I am independent, maybe a car, and especially, a bigger and better understanding of the English language. The problem of the visa was in the hands of other people, but a job and a house and bigger and better English—those problems are mine alone. As I ride buses up and down the streets of this big city full of cars and shops and milk bars, I look for places where I can apply for work. I begin to miss having my problems in the hands of others.

I gaze out of the window of the bus as if I were watching television. People here do not walk in the way they do in Afghanistan. Why is that? Is it because they know that bombs are not about to fall on them? They are not looking about quickly in the way people do in Mazar-e-Sharif. There is no danger in the air. It is as if the only things that happen here are the things that people expect to happen.

The clothing here is strange, also—I haven't yet become used to it. Nobody cares about clothing. They wear T-shirts and jeans and young boys wear baggy pants and the girls leave the middle of their bodies bare. If this were Afghanistan, every woman I see would be whipped and beaten, and most of the young girls with no clothing around the middle of their bodies would be put in jail or shot. The way people dress doesn't bother me, but it seems strange. I wish the young girls would not leave themselves so bare. They look cold.

The cars here—so many! And most have only one person inside. In Mazar-e-Sharif, cars are normally full of people.

Everything is ordered. The people of Dandenong are very obedient. When the traffic lights change to red, all the cars stop, and the people who are on foot cross the road. There are no policemen, no soldiers. The people obey the colours of the lights. I like it.

And something else I like is the light of the sky. It is almost summer now, and the sky is blue, a very strong shade of blue, very deep, the same as in Afghanistan. I like the trees, too. Even in the city where the traffic is heavy, I see trees along the side of the road. The blue sky behind the trees does something good to my heart.

I know that I will be happy to be in Australia in time. I know there are things that will please me every day. But just for now, my heart and head are full of anxiety. Employment is important. I know that I will relax once I am earning money. But how can I earn money? I pass a big building that looks like an office block. I cannot work in an office block. I pass a factory that makes carpets, but I have learned that Australian carpets are nothing like the carpets of my country. They come in big rolls—I have seen them in shops. They are made with machines. It would be mad for me to go into one of these shops and say, 'I am Najaf. I make carpets and rugs.'

Watching through the windows of the bus, I do not notice at first that a lady has taken a seat beside me. I do not notice until she says to me, 'And what part of South America are you from?' I have picked up enough English to understand her, but at the same time, I don't know why she has asked me this question. She is older than me, and seems very friendly. I reply with the words, 'I beg your pardon?' which I have learned to use often.

'What part of South America do you come from?' she asks again, speaking more slowly.

'South America?'

'Which country? Peru, maybe?'

'Peru? No.'

'Brazil?'

'No, no.'

'Chile?'

'Afghanistan.'

'Really? Afghanistan!'

We begin a conversation. This lady seems so eager to help me, and I am grateful. She asks me what work I do. When I tell her that I am a rugmaker, she is delighted. She tells me of a place in the city of Melbourne where Afghan rugs are sold; a place called High Street in an area called Prahran. She takes a pen and a notebook from her bag and writes down the name of the street and the area. She draws me a map, and explains it. She writes down the tram numbers and bus numbers. The words of English I am able to use are not plentiful enough to explain my gratitude to this friendly lady, but I try.

Prahran is not like Dandenong. The buildings are much older, and by the look of the shops, it is wealthier. I walk up and down High Street, glancing into the rug shops I find. Some of the rug shops please me; others look a little bit ridiculous, with Turkish, Persian, Afghan and Indian rugs all mixed up together. I enter one and find a woman inside – I must not say where she comes from or it will appear that I have a prejudice against her native land, and that is not true at all, or maybe it is true up to a point. This woman is only too happy to give me work once she learns that I am a skilled rug repairer.

'I have years of work for you!' she says. I am overjoyed, but perhaps a little too overjoyed, for as it turns out, this lady is a hard taskmaster. She pays me 12 dollars an hour—for me, a fabulous sum—but she demands that I work 12 hours a day, almost without stopping. I sit over the rugs, plying my tools, taking great care with my work, but I am always aware that her eye is on me. It's not a happy feeling, to have someone watching you constantly. Does she think I will stop work and wander about whistling songs?

But it's a job. I work according to her rules. In my mind, though, I am saying to myself, 'Lady, God help whatever poor man is your husband, for he must think of suicide each day of his life.' During my short lunch breaks, I go up and down High Street, leaving my mobile number (for indeed, I have a mobile phone, a wonderful instrument!) with the shop owners in case some extra work comes my way.

And extra work does come my way, thank God. I carry rugs back with me to the shared house in Dandenong on the tram and the train and the bus. A large rug can weigh 30 kilograms, and the task of carrying them is a struggle. I complain to myself, of course, for complaining is one of the great consolations for hardship provided by God, but I also remember the story of the wise camel: save your best complaints for the summit of the mountain ahead. In truth, I am beginning to see a long path stretching before me, and certainly there are mountain peaks to climb—finding a home, restoring my wife and child to me—but often in my day's work, even under the vigilant eye of the slave-driving lady, I find myself murmuring the words of songs from my native land. A path ahead is a great blessing. Also, being a practical person in many ways, I spend some of the money I have earned to purchase a small trolley, and now the trolley bears the burden of the rugs. God gave us burdens, yes, but God also gave us trolleys.

And today something has happened that makes me feel as if a great eagle has picked me up and carried me through the skies then returned me to earth as tenderly as a mother settling her child in its bed. I have found the wire brushes I need to comb the wool straight when I am repairing rugs. It is a crucial tool, and without it, I would never make much money from my craft. Here I stand in the middle of Prahran with my trolley laden with a big rug for repair. The need for a wire brush has become very pressing. And the type of wire brush I need is a most uncommon thing to come across. You cannot go to the supermarket and pick one up off the shelf. It is a specialist tool. I look east, I look west, then north, then south. Where on God's earth would I find this special brush? I may as well stand here with my hands outstretched and wait for someone to place one on my palm. Then I notice a second-hand shop just near the entrance to the train station. I push my trolley to the shop, make my way inside. A man, fairly old, quite friendly, asks me if he can help me. I describe as best I can the brush I am looking for, without any hope of finding one in here. The man takes four steps, reaches into a box and displays for me not one, but two of the very brushes I am searching for. I think to myself that what happened here this day is not real. It is as if I walked into a fruit shop and asked the greengrocer for a pomegranate grown on the slopes of a particular mountain in a particular land on the far side of the earth. And it is as if this greengrocer had said to me, 'It's funny you should ask, for two came my way just this morning.'

I stare at the brushes as if they were bars of gold. 'How much?' I ask the man.

'Ten dollars for the two,' he says.

I have only five dollars in my pocket, so I can afford only one. The man can see how longingly I watch him return the second brush to the box. Then he turns back to me and says, 'Are you a refugee?' I nod. 'Did I say ten dollars for two?' he says. 'No, I meant five dollars for two.' And he gives me the second brush.

If we wait a million years, we will meet two or three people of great generosity and kindness—people like the Prophet, people like the Jesus of the Christians, people like Gandhi, who is revered by the Hindus. The gifts these people bestow on mankind are great, surely. But we don't have to wait so long as a million years to meet people like the man in the second-hand shop who saw a path to kindness and took it. It is people like that man, and the lady on the bus, and many people I know in my native land who make the world possible; who keep things going while we wait for the one-in-a-million.

✳ ✳ ✳

I have said goodbye to the lady I had been working for. It was necessary. She treated me as if I had come from prison and would endure any sort of treatment just to keep my job. Nobody can keep his pride in such a situation. I have found a new employer, also in High Street, also from my region of the world. And he is no better than the woman. What has happened? Have all the business people of the Middle East who have a secret desire to own slaves come to live in Australia? Anyway, goodbye to this man, too.

Fortunately, I had met a man in the slave-driver lady's shop who has said he will help me. Why did he do this? Well, I helped him out with a rug that would not sit flat on the floor. Iron it, I told him. He said he'd tried that. I asked him, Did you iron the flesh or the bones? He looked at me as if I were mad and I explained to him, The front of the rug is the flesh, the back is the skeleton, so you fix the skeleton and the flesh will recover. Then I showed him; I ironed the back in a special way, and the rug sat flat, as it should. He was full of praise for me and asked me to ring him if ever I needed anything. And so I have phoned him and he has found me a new job with a salary in a carpet factory. It is my job to use a machine that cuts the pile of a rug evenly—and it happens that I am able to master this machine.

Earning a salary in this way, doing a job that I like well enough, has given me the first taste of security I have enjoyed in more than ten years. My employment in Mazar-e-Sharif was secure, yes, but my life wasn't. This is a lovely feeling, to be earning money and beginning to build. Daydreams turn into something firmer; around me a life is growing, just as a building grows. I like the people where I work. I tell the boss that I want to earn Halal money—that is, clean money—not Haram money—dirty money. What I mean is that I want my pay to be lawful, with taxes deducted; I do not want to be paid in some secret, no-taxation way, because this was suggested to me. If I am to do some justice to the decision of the Canberra Australians to let me stay in Australia, then okay, let me pay my share. I hope this makes the boss realise that I intend to be an honest man. It is an important matter to me to be understood in this way.

Today, trouble has blundered into my path. The supervisor of the factory sees me talking to an Egyptian man who has come and seated himself beside me while I work. The supervisor comes over and glares at the both of us. He takes the rugs I am working on and places them on the far side of the factory. 'Sit over here,' he says. 'Less talk, more work.' This makes me mad. What is this man suggesting? That I have become lazy? I walk straight to my locker, take my bag and head for the door. Suddenly the boss is chasing me. 'What's the trouble?' I explain to him, angrily, that my pride cannot bear being thought lazy—I would rather starve on the street than have a man standing over me and judging me unfairly.

The boss puts his hands on my shoulders, 'Everybody here trusts you, Najaf,' he says. 'Everybody respects you.' I can see that the supervisor is feeling that he may have made a mistake, and I accept the boss's apology. So I put my bag back in my locker and return to work. I think, 'Was I unreasonable? Did I do something foolish?' But I have to say no. At times in my life, I have had nothing to my name but my pride. It is the last thing I would ever give up.

18

Massacre

IN MY YEARS AS A shepherd boy, it was my task to keep the family's sheep alive. Sheep have no defences against predators. Their teeth can inflict no damage, they cannot run fast, and there is nothing about the look of them to make a truly wild creature draw back and think again before attacking. To impress on me the helplessness of the sheep in my care, my brothers told me shocking stories of sheep massacres; of wolves bounding down from the hills in a pack, maddened by the smell of the flesh they craved.

'When they come,' I was told, 'they leap great distances in their haste to devour their prey. They run like the wind with the moonlight shining in their eyes. They do not stop for a second when they reach the sheep, all huddled in fear—no, they tear through a whole flock in seconds, killing with a single snap of their jaws, ripping out the throats and bellies of the poor creatures. When they are done, blood is splattered over the pasture and hillside, even up the trunks of trees. Then the wolves fall on the youngest and most tender of the sheep and eat their fill.' Where did this story come from that my brothers terrified me with? It came from history, perhaps very ancient history. My brothers had never seen a pack of wolves bounding down from the hills but they had heard the story themselves when they were my age, and had passed it on to me to keep my mind on my job. But somewhere, at some time in the long history of Afghanistan, such a pack of wolves would have devoured a flock and some shepherd would have watched in horror. The story made a home in my mind, never to be forgotten. Sometimes as a boy when I sat eating my sandwich of bread and honey while the sheep grazed all around me, I thought of the wolves and laughed. Why should I fear them? The sun was shining, the breeze was blowing in the tall grass. This is a foolish story, I thought. The wolves will never come! But when it happened that I was guarding the sheep in the darkness of early morning, I believed in the wolves as fully as I believed in anything and my teeth chattered in my head.

The Taliban returned to Mazar-e-Sharif in 1998, and when they came, they came like the wolves in the ancient story. The first I knew of the attack was when I saw people, men and women and also children, running for their lives down Darwaza Shahidan boulevard and into the network of small streets near Bagh-e-Zanana Park. In Afghanistan, when you see people running you know that a disaster is about to strike, for nobody runs at any other time. It is our version of a siren, such as the one that sounds when a city is being bombed. If I had seen two or three young men running, I would have known that it was the army looking for people to enlist, but I saw hundreds of people running, mad with fear. I shrank back against a wall until I saw a man I knew, a friend of my brother Abdul Ali. I leapt out into his path and dragged him back into the shadows.

'What in the name of God is happening?' I asked him.

He looked wildly over his shoulder and struggled to get free of me.

'Taliban!' he cried out as he broke away.

I called to others as they streamed past and they shouted back, 'Taliban! They are killing Hazara!'

I was sick with dread. If the Taliban was already in the city, it meant that the Northern Alliance militias had already been swept aside. Nothing stood between the Hazara of the city and the vengeance of our enemy. I found a hiding place in a doorway down a narrow street and tried to think. The noise of automatic weapons fire was building into a roar, not like the brief bursts you would normally hear. That could only mean one thing: the Taliban were not fighting street to street, but were all firing at once on the Hazara they had rounded up. A massacre was taking place.

I remained where I was until the bombing began. I realised that the Taliban must have been herding people before them into the city centre, and now they were raining down mortar shells on the clogged city square. My hiding place was close to where the shells were landing. I heard screams, some of them were screams of terror, others were those of people who had been injured and were crying for help. I began to make my way back to our house, stopping every 20 metres to press myself against a wall. My nostrils were full of the smell that explosions make when concrete and brick are pulverised. People ran past me with their eyes wide, screaming as they ran. I recognised people I knew, but they were gone in a second.

I reached our house and hurled myself in through the door and onto the floor. My mother ran to me, perhaps not sure if I was dead or alive. She lifted my face in her hands and stared down at me, prayers streaming from her mouth.

'Run!' she said when she saw that I was breathing and uninjured. 'Abdul Ali has fled to Shar Shar.'

'Hakima and the baby?' I asked, for by this time my wife had produced a fine baby daughter, Maria. 'Where are they?'

'Hiding in the laundry. These devils won't kill women and children indoors unless they have no fear of God left to them. But they will kill you, surely. Run!'

I was on my feet and running within seconds. Outside, the noise from the city centre had grown louder still. The explosions pounded painfully against my eardrums. I did not run towards the road which would take me after many kilometres to Shar Shar, but towards the suburb of Yulmarab, where my friend, Ashraf had his house. If I had run down Darwaza Shahidan, I would have had to pass through the city centre, and I could not compel my legs to take that route. Wherever I turned, I came upon dead Hazara. Blood ran down the gutters and filled the gaps between the street cobbles.

I called to Ashraf from outside his door. I had to wait for a time before he opened the door and pulled me in; he was being cautious. His house was two storeys tall and, as I knew, he had made a secret room on the second floor when the house was built. This secret room was reached by descending a ladder through a trapdoor in the floor. The trapdoor had been fashioned so skilfully that no one could see its outline once it was closed. It had been made for just such an emergency as this, for the Hazara are a people who have lived with persecution and threats of sudden death for hundreds of years. The room was no bigger than a cupboard, but it was made to aid survival, not for comfort. Into this tiny space I clambered, together with my cousin, Gassem, the same age as me. There was no room for Ashraf himself, but he was not in such danger as Gassem and me as he was an old man. The oath of revenge the Taliban had sworn was against Hazara of fighting age, and although the bombing would certainly have killed many older men and women and children, we had some hope that when they took control of Mazar-e-Sharif and searched all the houses, they would spare women and children and men too old to have fought against them.

Gassem and I lay crammed together in that cupboard for 15 days. Sometimes in the darkness there was nothing to hear but the sound of Gassem's breathing, and my own. Or we might whisper to each other, to help give ourselves courage or simply to break the monotony. We spoke of our families, of our wives and children, of what we had seen on the streets before we had made our way into this small space, or we spoke of trivial, unimportant things just for the sake of using our voices; things such as where the best bread in Mazar-e-Sharif was baked, where the best pomegranates were to be purchased. Or we spoke of places we had visited, and of the beauty and splendour of Ali's tomb right here in our own city. At one time, I gave Gassem an account of the entire day of my marriage, including a description of each type of food served and each song played by the musicians. But there were times too, each day, when our voices broke into sobs.

When the women of the house whispered to us in our hiding

place that there was no one about, we would climb the ladder and stretch our limbs for a short time, then use the toilet and rapidly eat some food. We ate in the way that wild animals eat, with our ears pricked for the sound of our enemies.

Returning to the hiding place always made the sadness in my heart grow deeper still. I recall one time when I had been drowsing in the darkness and awoke with a great fear coiled in the pit of my stomach. Gassem was asleep. I listened and heard nothing but my cousin's breathing. It must have been night, with the women and children of the household themselves in bed and asleep. What am I doing here? I thought. I am hiding in a secret cupboard, a tiny space, and in all the vast area of my native land this is the only place where I can hope to escape my enemies. Could God have intended this? No, he did not intend it. He watches now with even greater sadness in His heart than I have in mine. He must be thinking, 'See what I provided! Soil and sunlight, pastures, mountains, rivers, trees, grain and fruit. And of this paradise, these people have made Hell.'

My friend himself was there one morning when we left the cupboard for some exercise.

'Ashraf, what news?' I asked him, but he shook his head. I asked again, and my friend raised his face and looked me straight in the eye. He told me of the fate of one of my uncles, and of that uncle's son, my cousin. The Taliban had driven them into a room of their house in the town of Shakh Abad, then thrown petrol everywhere, along the floor and the walls, over the rugs and the furniture. Then the Taliban soldiers struck a match, locked the door on my uncle and his son, and waited while they burned to death. Neither this uncle nor his son had ever fought the Taliban.

On the evening of the fifteenth day in the secret cupboard, I made a decision to return to my own home. I could no longer bear the torment of worrying about my mother and Hakima and Maria. There was something that I knew from stories my friend had told me: not every cadre of the Taliban would have been prepared to burn my relatives alive. Not every cadre would butcher innocent women and children. But many would, and I feared what fate would befall the women of my own household if the worst of the Taliban cadres went to my home.

I said goodbye to Ashraf, and to the women of his household. They blessed me, but their tears showed that they did not expect to see me alive again. I made my way through silent streets and rowdy streets like a stealthy creature of the wild, hugging the shadows. And I found my own home.

My mother was overjoyed to see me. She held my hands tightly, as if only the sense of touch would convince her that I was real, and not a phantom. Hakima, nursing the baby, looked at me with great sadness, as if she thought that my appearance in the house was intended only to wrench her heart all the more when the time came for me to leave again.

My mother told me that the Taliban had been making house-to-house searches in Hazara neighbourhoods, shooting young Hazara men on the spot, or sometimes taking them away with their hands bound behind their backs. She did not know if they would return to our house. They had been there twice already.

But we should have known that the Taliban soldiers would return. They are methodical people. They know nothing of the world, nothing of books and music, nothing of the pleasures of life, nothing of history, but they know how to find the enemies they seek. They came back within the week, and they took me.

Five Taliban soldiers kicked open the door and in seconds had placed themselves in the path of every exit from the house. One of the soldiers grabbed me by my throat and rammed me against a wall, the muzzle of his Kalashnikov resting on my cheek. I could see my mother's face over the shoulder of the Talib who was holding me. She had turned white.

'In God's holy name, spare my son!' she cried out. 'He is no fighter! He has never held a gun! I beg of you, spare my son!' Nobody said a thing in reply. The soldiers were looking not just for Hazara men, but for hidden weapons as well. They went rapidly from room to room, ripping apart furniture and throwing plates and bowls to the floor. One even went to the well in the courtyard, threw in a rope and climbed down to look for guns. He found nothing. Hakima and Maria remained well out of the way in a room upstairs.

The soldier who was guarding me lashed my hands behind my back and pushed me out into the street. There, on their knees, were five other men of my age, all with their hands bound, all of them Hazara. The expressions on their faces were those that you see on the faces of all men who have lost any say in whether they live or die: blank, but with terror seething behind the blankness.

All six of us were pushed into the back of a 4-wheel drive, encouraged to hurry with jabs of rifle barrels in our backs. Then the five Taliban soldiers climbed in, two with their weapons aimed at our faces. The driver took a route I recognised all the way to Dasht-e-Shour, where the Taliban had their command post. When we were unloaded from the 4-wheel drive, we were hurried forward into a big house that must once have been the home of a wealthy man, and then into a small room packed with other Hazara men.

All of us in that room—and our number was over 40, because I made a count in my first hour inside—expected to die, and feared not only our deaths, but the manner in which we would be killed. As captives of savage men, we were at the mercy of their mood. If one of the Taliban soldiers had lost a friend when Mazar-e-Sharif was first attacked a year before, who knows but that he may have a horrible vengeance in mind. I feared that we would all die in the way my uncle and cousin had died—burned alive in this room. Others in the room feared other fates, but no one I saw looked as if he was calmly resigned to death and pain. If anyone had walked past that big house not knowing what was happening inside, he would have guessed from the stench of fear that came off our bodies and rose into the air.

When we were first put into that room, we spoke quietly to each other, asking those around us to tell our families of our fate, should anyone survive. But after a time, we did not look at each other, as difficult as that was. People facing death are alone in the world, even when 40 of them are caged together. You cannot look into another man's eyes because you will embarrass him by witnessing his fear, and he will embarrass you by witnessing your own.

After hours had passed, Taliban soldiers stood at the door of the room and aimed their weapons at us while a commander demanded to know which of us had taken up arms 'against the defenders of the Faith.' It will not surprise you to learn that not one man was prepared to confess. The commander pointed here and there in the crowd and the soldiers seized those he'd pointed to, dragged them outside and beat them with whips fashioned

THE RUGMAKER OF MAZAR-E-SHARIF

from steel cable. All of us within listened to the screams with our heads bowed. Some men vomited where they stood. Others let their urine flow without shame.

When I was taken, I had said goodbye in silence to my family, to Hakima, to Maria. That was what I thought of as I waited for the soldiers to choose me: that I had said goodbye.

The Taliban soldiers threw me face down on the ground and flailed me with their whips. The pain of such a beating is so great that you are not aware of your own screams. You are not aware of anything but a few seconds of dread before the next blow lands on you. When I tried to wriggle away from the blows, I was kicked until I flattened my body on the ground again. I dug my fingers into the earth to hold myself still.

The Taliban commander shouted, 'Where are your guns? How many of us did you kill?'

I answered in the same way each time: 'I have never fired on anyone in my life. Walk down my street, ask anyone. I am a rugmaker, I am not a soldier!' I shrieked these words even when I had no faith left in the power of the truth.

None of us in that room escaped with just the one beating. As days passed, we were taken again and again. Waiting for the next beating is not like anything in life that I can suggest; it is not like a terrible toothache, it is not like severe depression, it is not like grief over the death of a beloved member of your family. Perhaps it is impossible to explain the feeling. 'Dread' and 'fear' would not convey what I mean. But I can say this: if it turned out to be true that Hell exists, and that servants of Satan do indeed whip us forward toward the furnace, and no tiny space in your heart or brain believes that you will somehow escape, that would be close to what it feels like to wait for a fresh beating with steel wire. At first I prayed to God, but only at first. I reminded him of the good things I had done in life, and promised with all my heart to do more good things if I were spared, and I reminded God, too, of the saying of our people, that a good deed is like throwing an object into the sea knowing that the waves will return it to you.

Our numbers in that room grew fewer as the days passed. Men who could bear no more beatings confessed to what they had not done—fought against the Taliban—in order to hasten death. Those who confessed were taken away and were not seen again.

How many days had passed before my final beating, I do not know. I was dragged out and whipped and answered the commander's demands with the same words I had started with. Then I was told to get to my feet.

'Get out of here,' said the commander, and he pointed at the gate. I staggered forward, not understanding what was happening but knowing enough to obey. Two guards unlocked the gate, then motioned me through. I was certain that I would be shot in the back of the head, even after I heard the gate lock behind me. After ten steps, after 100, I did not look around, still expecting to be shot. I looked at nothing except my hands, at my fingertips worn raw from clutching at the earth.

I walked in the rags of clothing on my body back to Mazar-e-Sharif.

19

Shop

THIS IS HIGH STREET, in the suburb of Prahran, in the city of Melbourne, in the state of Victoria, in the land of Australia. And this is my shop, the shop of Najaf Mazari, a shop where Afghan traditional rugs are sold and repaired and cleaned.

Except that there are no rugs to sell. The man in the second shop I worked in, before I took the job cutting pile, contacted me one day without warning and said he'd like to set me up in a shop. He had been very impressed by my knowledge of rugs. This was the most wonderful news, and I hurried up to High Street, found a vacant shop to lease, painted it in the gold and brown colours of Afghanistan, and then... nothing. The man let me down after building up my hopes. Now I have the rent to pay, and no stock to sell. Being the proprietor of a shop that has no opportunity to make me money is a strange feeling. I love the shop, but it is like having a ticket in a lottery: if it doesn't pay off, the ticket is just a piece of paper, and the shop is just an empty space.

I go down to the Housing Commission office in Prahran and ask for help to pay the rent. They can't help me because I am leasing business premises, not a house. I have an allowance from Centrelink that is not big enough to cover the rent. So my only option is to repair rugs day and night, sleep in the shop to save rent, and wait for Heaven to notice me, sitting lonely and miserable on the floor of my beautiful, empty, gold and brown shop.

The shop is not a very comfortable place in which to live, I must confess. I sleep on rugs out the back, make my food in a tiny kitchen. I have a sink where I can wash and clean my teeth, but no shower. I walk down to the council swimming pool in the early morning and pay for a shower there.

Sitting on the floor, with a rug on my knees that I'm repairing, I look up and gaze around, imagining the stock of rugs I would buy if I had the money. I would hang them from the walls, show them in the display window, spread them on the floor. I sigh and return to the repairs, whispering a prayer: 'God in your palace in Heaven, a few rugs for me to sell would please me more than I can tell you!'

We can never be sure when God is listening. Sometimes we shout at the top of our voices, and He makes no reply at all. But a whisper? Sometimes a whisper works better than shouting. An Afghani man has come into my shop, attracted by the gold and brown.

'Not much happening here, brother,' he says, and I explain the situation to him. I make him a cup of tea. We sit and chat. He asks me one hundred questions about rugs. Then he says, 'I'll supply the rugs, we split the profits.'

'You have rugs?' I ask in amazement.

'Many.'

'Where?'

'In my van.'

'Where is your van.'

'Out there.'

'Are you serious?'

'Yes brother, I am serious.'

He brings in armfuls of rugs. He shakes my hand. We sign nothing, but we each know that honour is better than paper. We make arrangements for more stock to be delivered. He leaves. A short time later, I sell two rugs. From this day on, all my prayers will be whispered.

I am making money, I have a business. Dear God, I think, let this not be a dream. But in truth, I know it is not a dream because even in my happiness, I am anxious and troubled. I found the land of Australia after a dreadful journey, I was given a visa, I found people of great generosity to help me, I found work, I found a shop, I found a man from my own country with a van full of rugs. But that visa of mine is a Temporary Protection Visa. The Canberra Australians can send me back to Afghanistan if they wish. Oh, it plagues me to think that in spite of all my struggle and all my good fortune, a man in a suit and tie sitting at a desk might one day say, 'Hmm, Najaf? Time for him to go back to Mazar-e-Sharif.'

One more whisper: Dear God, in your kindness, allow me to remain here.

* * *

I love my wife, I love my daughter, and I love the birds that come to the back of my shop for scraps of bread and biscuit. I have always loved birds. They are intelligent, they work hard to make a living, and they find time to sing. The birds must have Australian names, but I don't know what those names are. Some are small, some are big, all of them are friendly. They are not like the birds that we freed from the big cage at Woomera, but are still very beautiful in their own way. I throw the crumbs to them with a smile, and the smile stays on my face as they peck at the food.

Down at Prahran Market where I go each Saturday to buy vegetables and meat and cheese, small yellow canary birds are sold in cages – the same canary birds that I saw at Woomera. Each time I visit the market, I buy a canary bird in a cage and bring it back to my shop. First I watch the bird jumping about in the cage, and I whistle to amuse him, or maybe it is a her. Then I go to the back of my shop and wish the bird good fortune. I open the cage and let the bird fly away. It is so good for my heart! I see the bird fly swiftly to a tree or to the top of the fence, then he looks around as if he can hardly believe that he is free. Off he flies, I hope to a good life. Of course there is always the chance that a cat or even another bird will have him for dinner, but I am sure he would choose freedom, even if he knew the danger.

But being the God of the canary birds is not enough for me. I also free the fish I purchase from the pet shop in Chapel Street, not far from Prahran Market. I choose two or three small fish each week and carry them home in a plastic bag full of water. Later in the day, I walk to the Botanic Gardens with my plastic bag of small fish and stroll down the tracks between the trees. People pass me walking their dogs and look surprised to see me walking my fish. For that is what I tell people if they ask me: 'I am taking my fish for a walk.' And I tell them that it is the custom in my country. When I am away from all eyes, I creep down to the big lake in the Botanic Gardens and empty the fish into the water. They are gone in a second. Each fish has been granted a visa, by me. One time I saw the eels that live in the lake curling in the dark water, many of them together, and I was full of fear for the visa fish. But then I think, 'The fish must take their chances, like the birds.' Eels are everywhere, both in the world of fishes and in the world of refugees. The world was not fashioned by God to please me in every way. The fish have only a Temporary Protection Visa, just like me. The fish and Najaf share the same prayer: Do not let the eels devour us!

※　※　※

A new disaster to fix!

Just in these past two months, I have been able to telephone Hakima and Maria, who live in Pakistan over the border from Afghanistan. And I have been sending money to Hakima by paying it to a Pakistani in Melbourne, who then instructs a friend in Pakistan to pay it to Hakima. It was a complicated business contacting Hakima. The mobile telephone I call belongs to a family friend. When I call him, he searches for Hakima, and she talks to me. The line is not good, and we have only been able to shout such things as, 'I remain safe!' (from me) and 'When can we come?' (from Hakima). It is not possible to explain anything that requires more than four or five words. Hearing Hakima's voice and Maria's baby words flood me with happiness, in spite of all the shouting.

But now Hakima is angry with me. I have not been able to tell her about the clever invention I have at the shop, known as an answering machine. I have recorded a message on this machine in English: 'You have called Afghan Traditional Rugs. This is Najaf talking to you. I am not here. Leave a message and your number and I will call you back very soon.' But what do I find now? Hakima has been calling the number of the shop when it is daylight in Pakistan and night time in High Street, Prahran. She hears me on the answering machine and tries to talk to me in Dari, but what she hears is me saying in English, 'You have called Afghan Traditional Rugs. This is Najaf…' And she believes that I am refusing to talk to her in Dari. She believes that I have become so Australian that I scorn my native language. I learn all this from my friend. He tells me that my wife is refusing to speak to me. She says that she has enough to do without a husband by her side and no father there for her daughter, to also be learning English. She says that I am too famous in Australia to speak to her these days. 'Let me speak to her!' I shout, and she refuses.

I tell the story of the answering machine to my friend who owns the mobile phone. He asks me to explain again. I hear him calling to Hakima, 'It's a machine! It talks!' Then he asks me to explain a third time. Finally Hakima comes on the line, and I shout the same explanation to her in Dari. She says, 'Don't shout.' But she accepts what I say, and I tell her to allow for the time difference between Prahran and Pakistan, and I tell her exactly what the time difference is.

Peace, at last.

✳ ✳ ✳

The shop is too small for me to live in comfortably. In any case, did I find my way to Australia, to the suburb of Prahran to live in an area not much bigger than the cupboard in my friend's house in which I hid from the Taliban? I am making enough money now to have a home away from where I work. At Centrelink, they tell me to look in a part of the newspaper where people have rooms to rent in what are known as 'share houses'. I lived in a share house in Dandenong. I know what is required.

I put a mark against all the share houses near Prahran and ring them on my mobile. The first one I try says, 'Ask for Heather', so when the phone is answered, I say, 'I want to speak to Heather.'

'This is Heather,' says a voice.

'You have a room?'

'Maybe.'

'Maybe?'

I don't know what she means. I can hear music playing.

'We're looking for a student, probably,' Heather says.

'Good! I am a student!'

This is true. I am studying English at the Swinburne school.

'Okay, cool. How old?'

'How old is what?'

'You!'

'Me?'

'Yeah. But look. I don't think this is going to work.'

She hangs up.

The next one is also a girl. Even before I can say more than two words, she says, 'Smoke free, you realise.'

'Pardon?'

'Smoke free. It says in the ad.'

She is right. It says, 'Smoke Free Household'. I have no idea what that means.

'Are you a smoker, if you don't mind my asking?'

'You mean cigarettes? Certainly. Dunhill in the red box.'

'No can do. Sorry.'

'You don't like cigarettes?'

'Smoke free.'

'Okay. I smoke outside.'

'There's still toxins in your lungs. I have to say no.'

The next one is answered by a woman who sounds angry before I say a thing. She says, 'Look, can we get it clear right off about being vegetarian? Vegetarian means vegetarian; fish are not vegetables, chickens are not vegetables, okay? I've had about a hundred calls from people who *think* they're vegetarians.'

This is completely baffling to me. What in God's name does she mean? What is 'vegetarian'? I saw it in the ad, but I didn't take it seriously.

'Hold on for one minute?' I say, then run next door to talk to the man in that shop. I know him quite well.

'David,' I ask him, 'what is this?' I show him the ad with the word 'vegetarian' in it.

'No meat,' says David, 'only vegies.'

'Pardon?'

'People who only eat vegetables, my friend. Wankers, mostly.'

'People who only eat vegetables? Are there such people?'

'Oh, yeah. All the go, in certain circles. Wankers.'

'No meat?'

'Nope. Maybe a bit of fish now and again.'

'She says no fish.'

'Wankers. Might be one of them vegans.'

'Vegans? What is vegans?'

'Only eat vegies, nothing else. No cheese. Maybe a few apples. Wankers.'

I run back to my mobile and say, 'Yes, I am vegetarian.'

'Absolutely?'

'No,' I say. I have changed my mind.

'That's what I thought.'

At last I find a room with a Muslim couple who have a restaurant in Prahran. The room is above the restaurant and very, very noisy at night. But I can put up with the noise. The room has a shower. I love having a shower in my own room. I stand and stare at it in wonder, just for the pleasure it gives me.

Very good things are happening. My family was right. I am lucky. But days come along, such as this day, when I feel like sitting and staring at the sky with a hand on my heart. I am glad about Australia, but can I ever feel the truth about myself in Australia? The truth about being Afghani? In Mazar-e-Sharif, many of the people I saw each day were my relations; here, there is only me. This is hard to explain, but I don't feel as if I have brought my whole body to Australia. I have my own skin, but what is inside is not Najaf. I have my own brain, but much of what my brain contains is asleep. In your own country with your family nearby, each part of you fits together. Here, parts of me don't know how to join up with other parts. And more than that, in Afghanistan everybody understands me. Just by looking at me, an Afghani knows a thousand things about me, and about any other Afghani. By looking at me, my family knows even more about me; ten thousand things. Here, people know maybe one thing, maybe two things, at best three things about me. I was used to people knowing me, and I find it hard to get used to people not knowing anything about me but my shape. People can see that I am a Muslim, for example, but that doesn't explain anything about me. What sort of a Muslim am I? What parts of my religion—and there are many, many parts— do I hold closest to my heart? If you put ten Muslims together, you have ten different ways of being a Muslim. Everybody knows this in Afghanistan. Nobody knows it here.

But enough. I am very reluctant to talk about things that trouble me when there is so much that gives me joy. It is important to me that I am making friends in Australia—Australian friends. This lady who stands before me now looking at cushion covers—she will be my friend, I can tell. I chat with her for an hour, and learn that she is a teacher of the English language, although she is retired. As soon as she tells me that she teaches the English language, a plan comes into my mind, but I don't say anything about it just for the moment. She is very friendly, in the way that Australians are. She is interested in Afghan rugs. Of course, I have met many friendly people, but Robin is different. I like her, and everything about her. I tell her to take the cushion covers with her and see how they look in her home. She is pleased that I trust her. People always like being trusted.

For me, running a business in Australia is like having two full-time jobs at once. The first job is selling rugs, repairing rugs, cleaning rugs, keeping my shop full of stock. The second job is working for the government, or for two governments— the government of this state of Victoria in which I live, and the government of the whole of Australia in the city of Canberra. Papers come for me in the mail almost every day. This paper says, 'Understanding GST'. I tried to read it, but I need a second paper called, 'Understanding the first paper'. On my desk I have another paper: 'What you need to know about BAS'. And another: 'Workplace Safety'. And another: 'Compulsory Superannuation'. And another: 'PAYG and Accountability'. And another: 'WorkCover, Employer Obligations'. And another: 'ATO Guide, Annual Reporting Option B'. And another, and another, and so on. I sit at my desk at the back of my shop and stare at the papers. They make me think of seagulls when you are on the beach at St Kilda, as I have been. You are trying to eat your fish and chips, and the seagulls gather all around you, each one wanting some of your food. You chase them away, but they come back again in less than a minute. Business is much easier than this in Afghanistan. A man buys a rug from you and gives you money. That is the end.

I have an Australian friend called Colin who is an auctioneer. He sells my rugs up at Malvern Town Hall when there is a big auction day. He tells me, 'You need an accountant, mate.' Well, I know what an accountant is; even in Afghanistan, we have one or two accountants. But surely this will cost me a great deal of money? I worry about it for days, staring at the pile of papers on my desk. Finally, my friend Aljaf who also sells rugs tells me of an accountant, but he doesn't tell me how much this man will charge me. I hire this accountant, but he has a look about him that worries me. I fear a huge bill to put on top of all my other papers soon. I must have a worried look on my face, because a customer has just asked me what is troubling me. She is a Maori lady, a fine person. 'This!' I say, pointing at the papers. 'I have an accountant to help me now, but I think he is going to ask me for more money than I have.'

'Calm yourself, Najaf, life is too short.'

We sit and drink tea. I am calm now. Barbara says, 'I'm going to bring my partner here. He'll do your accounts. It will cost you nothing, I promise. Can you afford nothing?'

'Really?'

'Really and truly,' says Barbara.

My next crisis is the crisis of the plastic cards. I have been running my business as a cash business, but often people come in and find a rug they like and want to pay me with a plastic card. I have to say no, and it embarrasses me and deprives me of business. People look at me as if I have come from the Stone Age when I tell them that I don't know anything about cards.

Colin, the auctioneer tells me, 'Go to the bank, mate. Get a machine.' So I go to the bank and sit down with a man who says he wants to help me. 'I need a machine,' I tell him. 'A machine that makes money from plastic cards.'

'EFTPOS is what I think you're talking about. Not a problem. How long have you been in business?'

'Four months.'

'Ah, well, right there we run into trouble, I'm afraid. You need to be in business for six months before you can perform EFTPOS transactions.'

Now, this is a day on which my temper is not so good. And my patience is not so good, either. The man who is interviewing me is smiling, as if the 'trouble' he is talking about is of not much concern to him. But it is of great concern to me.

'I came here from Afghanistan,' I tell him. 'In my country, there is no plastic money...'

The smiling man interrupts me to say, 'Transaction cards, is what we call them in Australia.'

'Okay, but you know what I'm talking about. None in

Afghanistan. Here, people come into my shop every day. They want to buy rugs. I have the most beautiful rugs in the land of Australia. They show me a plastic card. I have to say no. I look foolish.'

'Not to worry,' says the smiling man. 'Two more months, come back and see us.'

'I can't wait two months. Do you want my business to disappear? I need a machine!'

'Yes, but as I explained…'

'No, don't explain. Give me a machine! Please.'

So the smiling man goes away and talks to another man. I wait. Smoke is coming out of my ears. The smiling man comes back, but he is not smiling now.

'Now, Mr Muzbari…'

'Mazari. My name is Mazari.'

'Sorry. Mr Mazari, I think we may be able to help you.'

And so I get my machine. It comes with a book of instructions. I try to read the book, but it is not an easy book to understand. The next time a customer gives me a plastic card, I ask him to read the book and work the machine. I tell him that I grew up in a place where people still bury their money in the ground instead of going to the bank. This is not true, but I am trying to make a joke. Making jokes in English is not so easy for me. I don't want to make a mistake. I study English at the Swinburne school, and my friend Robin also teaches me English at her home and cooks meals for me and listens to my troubles. She is like a mother to me. I remember times when I was in such despair in Afghanistan, and on my journey to Australia. If I had known that at the end of my journey, I would find such a friend as Robin, I would have thought all the pain and fear was worthwhile for such a reward.

20

Exile

WHEN I HAD REACHED my home after being released by the Taliban, my mother stared at me as I stood in the doorway. She took one, two, three steps back until she was standing against the wall. Her hands went to her face and a cry came from her such as I had never heard her utter in her life, not even when Gorg Ali died, not when the rocket landed on our house, not even when she fell from the roof of our house and hurt herself so badly. I think she did not know for a minute or more if I were her living son or his ghost. For my part, I stood motionless where I was, perhaps as unsure if I were alive or dead as my mother was. Then my mother came quickly across the floor to me and put her hands on my face as tenderly as if she were holding a wounded bird. Tears ran down her cheeks, but she was silent.

'Is it you?'

I didn't answer, but I took her hands and held them in mine. My mother looked down and saw the raw flesh of my fingertips. She touched my face again. We stood together in silence for what seemed such a time, and in all that time I had no desire to move from where I stood, not until Hakima came into the room.

Being freed by the Taliban once did not mean that they had ceased to take an interest in me. They were interested in all the Hazara, especially in men of my age, and the thing they were most interested in was killing us. Over the weeks that followed my release, I remained in the house, dreading the sound of a rifle butt on the front door. In the city, more young Hazara men had been taken away and executed. My friend Yassim was amongst those taken—I had known him since boyhood. He was a fine young man, loyal and kind. It seemed to us that the aim of the Taliban was genocide. They would begin with the young men, then move on to the older Hazara, and when the children were old enough to be killed, surely they too would die.

Staying in the one place, even in hiding, would end with me being found. Perhaps I would walk outside one day when I thought the Taliban were not watching and somehow be noticed. Or the Taliban soldiers would take it into their heads to search every square inch of my home, and so discover me. I made a decision to keep on the move, going from village to village in the north and north-west by bicycle, living on the little money I had saved. It was a desperate plan, but at that time we still hoped that the Taliban would depart from the north. It was a question of outlasting them.

I rode all day sometimes, always heading into regions where the Taliban were weakest. My path nearly always led me uphill into the mountains and the cycling was hard going. At night

I stayed in mosques or slept outside under a tree or in a field, always as wary as a wild animal that was being hunted. Even after the effort of cycling for the whole day, I slept lightly. A stone rolling down a slope half a kilometre away was enough to wake me, or the crack of a twig falling from a tree.

Now and again I risked sleeping in a serai, a simple inn where travellers sleep together all in one room. I never felt in danger of betrayal by the ordinary people of the regions I travelled in. The people of the north were no friends to the Taliban. But it was always possible that a Taliban patrol would stop and check the serai, so I could never relax. I chose a spot, each time, that gave me a clear sight of all approaches to the place where I lay.

When you are the prey of a force you cannot hope to match in strength, your body uses every particle of strength to keep you alive and alert. There is no strength left over. Worrying would take strength, so you cease to worry about anything but the minute that lies before you. But as I came to understand, this type of vigilance is wearing away something inside, for the soul reaches a stage when it rebels and cries out to you, 'Enough! You are a human being! I will not accept this life of an animal one day longer!' This voice called out to me in that way one morning when I was making my way uphill, walking beside my bike because the grade was too steep. I stopped and closed my eyes. I tried to resist the voice. It was futile. How can you resist what your soul itself is saying? I opened my eyes and looked down at the valley below, at the bright thread of the river and the green fields of the flood plain. I recognised the picture below me. I was close to my home village of Shar Shar. Without knowing, I had been cycling for the past few days towards my birthplace.

I cycled into my village in the afternoon. There were few signs of the Taliban, who kept their distance from such a stronghold of the Hazara. I spent a few days cautiously working out what dangers I would face before merging into the village life. And it was a sad village I had returned to. The Taliban did not patrol the village all that frequently, but their police nevertheless insisted on the populace keeping the rules of the regime. Women were confined indoors unless accompanied by an adult male. A strict dress code was in force, requiring those women who could venture outside to dress in the old-fashioned burka that left no patch of skin visible. No wonder such sadness hung in the air! Restrictions such as those the Taliban enforced are hateful to the Hazara. We wish to see women educated, we are proud of our tolerance not only within our own religion but of other religions as well. We say this about our women: an uneducated father is a pity, but an ignorant mother is a tragedy.

In Shar Shar, I was able to live in the houses of people who knew my family well from the days when we lived there. My brother Gorg Ali who died just outside Shar Shar was still honoured greatly in the village, and people were very glad to assist me. I stayed for some days in one house, then moved to another so that the burden should not fall all on one household. Also, people wanted to show me generosity, and it was only polite to move from place to place.

Traffic passed between Shar Shar and Mazar-e-Sharif each day: trucks and cars, people on motorcycles. News was carried between the village and the city in this way and word reached me in Shar Shar that my family had made a plan. I was summoned to a secret meeting in the village, attended by my brother

Abdul Ali, a number of cousins and two uncles. I was to leave Afghanistan and travel to a country in the West where I might be accepted as a refugee. The family would find the money by emptying their pockets and retrieving banknotes from hiding places and selling what could be sold. The sum required, as we knew, was 3,500 American dollars. Such a sum would pay a people smuggler. My family and friends could not have afforded more than one payment to a people smuggler.

The money they raised used up every tiny piece of cash they could find, and left their houses bare of things to sell. I was the chosen one, but the reasons were practical and had nothing to do with them loving me best, or anything like that. I was the family member most in danger; I was also the only one with a few words of English to employ, picked up from a friend in the rug factory; and on top of that I was judged the most level-headed person in the entire family, moderate when it came to religion, never involved in fighting or politics. Finally, I was considered lucky. I had survived the rocket attack, I had managed to keep out of the hands of the militias enlisting men and boys in their armies, and I had come back from the dead after falling into the hands of the Taliban. To reach a country in the West where I would be permitted to stay as a refugee would require a great deal of luck. The possibility of me being captured along the way was very high.

My family wanted to save my life before anything else, but there was another reason they gave up all their hard-earned savings to send me to safety. Afghanistan is a nation, and within that nation there are ethnic groups of various sizes, and within those ethnic groups, such as the Hazara, there are large tribes, and within those large tribes there are smaller tribes, and within

220

those smaller tribes there are smaller tribes still—the tribe of a man's family, including the father and usually more than one mother, aunts, uncles, first and second cousins and in-laws. This family tribe can easily number one hundred. Afghanis want to see their nation survive, but if it cannot, they want to see their ethnic group survive, but if it cannot, then let the larger tribe survive, and if not then at least the smaller tribe, and if the smaller tribe cannot survive, then let God grant that the family tribe will remain on earth, and prosper at some future time. And this is where I come in: if the family tribe cannot survive, then by the mercy of God, let one male member of that tribe find safety in the world, and let him rebuild everything from the start, so that in one hundred more years or even in one thousand years, the land of Afghanistan will return to the map with the Hazara living in their traditional regions and a house in Mazar-e-Sharif filled with the descendants of Najaf and Hakima.

To leave your native land is a terrible thing. People all around you might wish to shoot you through the head and throw your body in a ditch, but still, it is a terrible thing to turn your face away from your own land. If I could remain alive in Afghanistan in poverty, searching each day for food for my wife and children and myself, dwelling in a shelter that barely kept the rain and the sun and the snow off our heads, I would have stayed. I had remained when the Russians and the communists fought the mujahedin. I remained when the mujahedin fought each other. I remained when one president after another took his seat in the Kabul palace. I remained when the Taliban came to power. I remained when those same Taliban chased my kinsmen and friends through the streets of Mazar-e-Sharif and shot them down like animals. But I could not remain any longer, because that would be suicide. The Taliban would find me again and surely kill me.

I travelled secretly back to Mazar-e-Sharif with a truck driver. There, with great sorrow in my heart, I arranged for my wife and baby daughter to travel to safety in Pakistan, prepared what documents I could, put on clean clothes, embraced each beloved member of my family and with tears running down my cheeks, began my journey.

21

Home

I HAVE SPOKEN OF times when I am broken apart by grief and sorrow, but have I mentioned often enough those times when I am wild with joy? Such a time has come my way. The Canberra Australians have told me in writing that I can remain here forever. I have the document before me. I gaze at the words, 'Permanent Residency Status' with a smile on my face that makes my jaw ache. Are there more beautiful words in any document anywhere on earth? Let me speak them aloud:

'Permanent Residency Status.'

They go to my heart, like the voice of God answering a prayer. *Permanent Residency Status*. And I think of what this will lead to: a reunion with Hakima and Maria!

Now and then I have seen signs on the windows of the neighbouring shops here in High Street written by the proprietor; signs that say, 'Back in 5 minutes', and 'Closed for one hour due to family crisis', and also, 'Closed due to illness'. I feel like writing a sign to put on the window of my own shop; a sign written in gold and brown in letters a metre high. And this sign would say: 'Closed due to the happiness of Najaf Mazari'.

This night my friend Robin is making a party for me at her house. All my friends are invited, as is both natural and wonderful. I do not drink alcohol, but I can be very drunk without liquor. I am drunk now. Let my friends beware, let Robin beware! I may sing very loudly and for a long time. *Permanent Residency Status*. Dear God, my gratitude forever.

❉ ❉ ❉

New things continue to happen for me. The new project for my brain is to understand the computer. I have a computer now, and I have had some lessons. I love the computer. It is the most beautiful machine ever invented in the history of the world. Look, I press here and—incredible—all my sales for the past two months! And look, look further, this is amazing and wonderful. I go into the search engine, okay, I press here, I press here, I write: www.afghantraditionalrugs.com.au. Wait just a few seconds. And see, this is my own website, if you can believe such a thing. My friend designed it for me. Pictures of rugs, pictures of me working, prices, information about rugs. Everything. And it is mine. Can you imagine this? Have you ever seen anything more wonderful? But there is much more for me to understand. I want to learn how to make links. Links are very important. That is my project now—learning about links.

It is important for me that the computer occupies my brain. It is good for business, of course, but while I am sitting in my chair that turns when I turn, using my fingers on the keyboard, I am able to stop thinking about anything else for a short time. A great sorrow has come into my life, the death of my friend Ali Sarwari. He made a journey from Afghanistan to Australia to escape the Taliban, just as I did, and when we met in Australia, we knew within ten seconds that we would be friends for all our lives. It was not just that we shared the same language and the same experiences in our homeland; no, for me at least, it was to do with Ali's kindness and courage, which I could see in his face and especially in his smile. And how much courage he needed, for his wife and brother and daughter were kept by the Canberra Australians on a strange island in the ocean, an island that was like Woomera where refugees lived behind a wire fence. The Canberra Australians believed that the Taliban would kill him if he went back to Afghanistan, but his wife and brother and daughter they would not accept. It is madness, but amongst the Canberra Australians there are madmen, as well as those who are generous and wise.

Ali helped me in my business, and made it possible for me to order large shipments of rugs from Afghanistan to offer to my customers. Ali's face was made for smiles, and he smiled all the time. Only a few people knew of his grief as he imagined his family being sent back to Afghanistan in an aeroplane. What happiness can you enjoy when your wife and daughter and brother live on a strange island in the ocean, and cannot share your life? Then the government of New Zealand said they would accept Ali and his whole family, and he travelled to the city of Hamilton and made his home there. For three years, he was the happiest person on earth. Then this disaster that has torn my heart: a car crash in New Zealand near the city of Auckland has killed my friend. I wept for him with my hands over my face when I heard, and I wake in the mornings with the same grief in my heart and the same tears on my cheeks.

The computer distracts me briefly from my sorrow, but it is my friend Robin on whom I depend for true comfort. She has become a second mother in my life. If I had to choose one person, one Australian I could show to everyone I know in Afghanistan and say, 'This country in which I live and work has such fine people as this wonderful woman to welcome strangers such as me,' it would be Robin I would choose. She listens to me in times when happiness has made me crazy with joy, and in times when I grieve for reunion with my wife and daughter. God's blessings on her.

22

Journey

THE MAN WHO ARRANGED my escape from Afghanistan was a Pashtun by the name of Qadem. Hazara and Pashtuns have never been friends. Pashtuns for centuries have made life as miserable as they possibly could for the Hazara. It was they, the Pashtuns, who took the traditional lands of the Hazara and distributed them amongst themselves, and it was the Pashtuns who attempted to force their Sunni religion on the Hazara. Our grievances with the Pashtuns go back a very long time into history. So it made me anxious that it was into the hands of a Pashtun that I was entrusting my life. But at least Qadem knew me. We were not strangers. He knew that I worked as a rugmaker, he knew that my family was not involved in fighting the Taliban (most of whom were Pashtun) and he knew, too, that I would surely be killed if I remained in Afghanistan. I was a human being in his mind and heart, not just a nameless Hazara.

Even so, he was not friendly towards me in the least. He did not treat me badly, but nor did he try to set my mind at rest. Perhaps that was a greater sign of trust than if he'd said, 'No, no, don't worry about anything, I will never betray you.' He only ever led me to believe that he was an ill-tempered man who had little time for the Hazara. That is not the strategy of someone who intends to hand you over to your enemies.

On a certain day, Qadem summoned me to his house and dressed me from head to toe in the white robes and white turban of the Taliban. With a scarf drawn across my mouth, no one would know without checking more closely that I was Hazara. Then he disappeared for a short time and returned in a 4-wheel drive, very like the one in which the Taliban had taken me away months earlier. Inside the vehicle, packed together, were twenty more men dressed in just the way I was—that is, dressed as Taliban. Those reading my story will imagine the fear running through me when I glanced inside at people dressed like those who wished to put me to death. Nevertheless, I climbed into the vehicle and forced myself into a seat.

I did not meet the eyes of any of the others within. Some of them might have been people I knew, but it was as if all of us had decided that silence was best. It was also possible that some of these people were real Taliban; that we were a mixture of true fanatics and pretenders. For all I knew, Qadem was intending to deceive us.

Qadem drove south, through Pol-e-Khomri and Durahy Bamiyan. Along the way we were forced to stop at Taliban checkpoints, and at each stop, Qadem left the 4-wheel drive and spoke in Pashtun to the guards. What he was saying was a mystery to me. Perhaps he was saying, 'I have a truckload of believers heading for Pakistan.' Or he may have said, 'Don't check these people too closely, and there will be a present for you by-and-by.' The Taliban were supposed to be too pure to take bribes, but perhaps they were not quite as pure as they claimed.

In any case, with my heart full of dread, I had no energy left to me to work out what Qadem's real plans were. I prayed to God that Qadem would not deliver me to the Taliban, and after ten checkpoints, it seemed to me that he was keeping his end of the bargain. I didn't look out the windows. This was not a holiday.

The last checkpoint inside Afghanistan was at the border post. If there was to be a thorough search of the 4-wheel drive, this was where it would happen. But we passed through without trouble, and into Pakistan and on to the city of Peshawar—a city full of Afghani refugees fleeing the Taliban, but also full of Taliban. But the Taliban did not have the right to arrest me or murder me here in Pakistan. Once we left the vehicle at the train station, I was free to remove the white robes. It was only then, when I was myself again, that the pain of leaving my country came upon me. What I was doing seemed madness, in certain ways. I had only one homeland, and I had abandoned it. If I travelled all over the world, I would never find another Afghanistan. I put my hands to my face and wiped my wet cheeks.

The train journey from Peshawar to Karachi is long and slow. I stayed with those who had travelled with me in the 4-wheel drive. All were present, so perhaps none of them had really been Taliban. I saw the names of the stations as the train pulled in, but was unable to read them. One of our number who could, murmured the names to us: Daud Khel, Mianwali, Leiah, Mutan, Khan, Sukkur, Khaipur, Hyderabad, and finally, Karachi.

There was little time to rest in Karachi before we were driven to the airport to catch the jumbo jet to Jakarta, in the land of Indonesia. It was at this time that it was whispered to me that our final destination was to be Australia. It meant nothing. When I crossed the border into Pakistan, that was the first time I had left my native land. I had no knowledge of the world. I knew that America was very rich and not a land of Muslims, but Australia? I had heard of a creature called a kangaroo that leapt instead of running or walking, and I knew that this strange animal had something to do with Australia, and that was all. If we were going there, it must be a wealthy land. For all I knew, it was part of America.

In Jakarta, it was necessary to wait for the boat that would take us to Australia. The people who were managing things told us little. When we asked how long we would have to wait, they shrugged. If we said, 'More than a week?' they still shrugged. What I noticed was that they cared for us in the group very, very little. They didn't even look at us as if we were people who breathed and thought and had feelings. We were cargo, like sacks of wheat. Perhaps they expected that we would all die, anyway. Nothing good can happen to your soul when you deal with human beings like sacks of wheat. But should I even think that? Was it they who asked me to run from the Taliban? I thought to myself, 'Najaf, they do what they are paid to do, and it is lucky for you they do it at all.'

I saw Jakarta only a little. It was nothing like anything I had experienced before. These people were Muslims like me, but so different in the way they dressed and walked and chattered. And so many of them in the busy streets! The air smelt different, too. The heat of the air was not like the heat in Mazar-e-Sharif in summer. The foods that left their aromas in the air were puzzling to me. And this land of Indonesia was only one of very many lands in the world! For the first time, I began to think of how vast this earth must be, and how it must be home to people I could hardly imagine. I don't think that I had known before I came to Jakarta that the world was truly real. But even though Jakarta and this new part of the world were fascinating to me, I could not behave like a tourist. I was aware all the time that I was only part of the way through a desperate journey that might still end in disaster. I was like a child who is having a story in a book read to him; a frightening story of monsters and catastrophes. The child wishes to listen, but his fear makes him put his hands over his eyes sometimes, or over his ears. That is how I saw Jakarta—like a child peeking out through his fingers.

I was told eventually to meet the organisers of the smuggling operation at a certain place and at a certain time. I made sure I was where I was supposed to be at exactly the right time. A crowd of people had gathered—all of them fleeing their lands. I heard Arabic being spoken, Dari, Farsi and languages that were a mystery to me. As we waited for more directions in the dark of night, I thought of the strangeness of this whole business. All of us were moving in fear and secrecy from different parts of the world in search of another part of the world where we could be relaxed and happy. We were like a small tribe, driven from our homes, heading for a place we knew nothing about except that our enemies could not find us there. This is how my distant ancestors came to Afghanistan.

Our small tribe was moved about by bus and ferry to a small town on the coast called Baubau. A further bus ride took us away from all habitation to a place on the coast where a small jetty reached out into the sea. Tied up at the jetty was a wooden boat that even in the faint light of early morning looked about to fall to pieces and sink. The boat had only a single deck topped by a small, ramshackle structure like a hut. At first, I thought this was a fishing boat of some sort, left to rot where it had ended its life. It did not occur to me that all of us in this tribe of mine would be asked to climb on board. But that is exactly what the people smugglers told us to do. We stood in disbelief with our bundles beside us, some of us with children squatting in the sand. I smiled at first, for surely this was a joke. But the people smugglers urged us forward onto the jetty. One of them was trying to explain in a mixture of Dari and Arabic that another, bigger boat would meet us out at sea. He made gestures with his hands to impress on us how much bigger the boat that was waiting would be. We had to believe him. If he had said, 'This boat will take you to Australia,' I think we would have all run off into the jungle and taken our chances with the wild animals.

Ninety-six of us boarded the boat. I was amongst the first, and as more and more people followed, the boat sank lower in the water. By the time everyone was on board, the waterline had crept dangerously close to the deck. The deck itself was as crowded as a railway platform, like the one in Karachi. Children clung to their mothers, fearing the journey ahead. I had time to look below deck before the engine started, and what I saw made my heart sink lower than the boat. It was a slum down there. A single oil-burning stove was all that was provided for cooking, and on that stove only one pot could be heated at a time. The dirty straw-filled mattresses on the floor made up the sleeping accommodation, apart from the pallets on deck. The whole below-deck section of the boat stank of diesel fuel and fish. Breathing in that stench almost made me sick before the journey had even started. But this was the first boat I had seen in my life, other than the derelict ferries that had transported us part of the way here from Jakarta. For all I knew, this was what most boats were like. Still, gazing about me as people shouted and clambered about on the deck above, I knew that we would need the help of God to survive for long on the open sea.

We headed away from the jetty and out to sea with a prayer on the lips of every passenger, and probably the captain prayed, too. The sea was calm this close to land, however, and as the sun rose, the horizon appeared in the far distance. I stood on the deck near what I now know is called the bow of the boat (at the time, I called it the pointed end) and watched the water shearing away on both sides as the vessel forged ahead. The racket of the engine was like that of an ancient truck climbing a steep hill, and diesel smoke and fumes filled the air. I had every reason to feel dread, but instead my heart was lifted up and filled with hope. For this was my first view of the ocean, and it thrilled me and almost made me weep. Such beauty! I came from a land that has no coastline at all, and I had wanted to see such an ocean as this ever since I was a boy. I had been shown a globe of the world in school, and the teacher had explained the blue paint to us: 'It is water, but full of salt.' And that was true, but he had said nothing about the wonder of it.

On the first day out at sea, the captain told us to form groups of ten and elect a leader for each group. I was asked to become the leader of one group, made up mostly of Afghanis, but including one Iranian. My tasks, as I was told by the captain, were to make sure that everyone got a fair share of food, did a fair share of the cleaning work, and obeyed the rules. The rules were all to do with behaving peacefully and honestly. These rules of the captain's were a little bit comical coming from him, because he didn't impress me as being peaceful or honest. But I could see the point of having rules and was content to take on the responsibilities of group leader. Why not? I like peace and I like honesty.

It did not take many days of sailing before the desperation of what we were doing began to shorten people's tempers. The food was boring, just rice and potatoes, with hard biscuits and black tea at breakfast time and again at night. To cook for 96 people on one small stove took two hours or more, with first one group then another taking its turn in what was known as the galley. The toilet was right next to the galley and whenever a woman needed to use the toilet while food was being prepared, all the men had to leave the below-decks area, letting the cooking wait. After three days, the stink of the toilet had begun to mix with the stink of the engine fumes, and the smell was almost enough to make us all faint.

I think it was after we'd been at sea for a week that we understood, each one of us, that we would not be meeting up with another, bigger boat. Whenever we asked the captain about the bigger boat that had been promised, he denied any knowledge of it. Way out in the ocean is not the place to have an argument with the only person on the boat who had ever sailed out on the ocean before; the only person who knew how to find a path over the waters. I grumbled, and that was all, when the captain said to me, 'What boat? I know nothing of another boat.' The beauty of the ocean began to fade for me when I became sure that our only hope for this new life we all so deeply desired depended on this stinking vessel staying afloat.

At certain times in the first ten days, we had glimpsed islands and even seen the faint outlines of big ships on the horizon. But after those ten days, we saw nothing. I often sat on the deck where the air was freshest and gazed straight ahead. All around me, Afghanis, Iranians, Chechens and Iraqis groaned with seasickness or other even worse illnesses, or else complained about hunger, or cursed the filthiness of our vessel, or wept in frustration. The sun shone down on us so fiercely that it felt as if the wooden boat would burst into flame. Mothers kept their children covered as best they could. Those on deck would sometimes take a short holiday from the heat of the sun by going below deck, but the heat was just as bad down there and the stench unbearable.

Sitting on deck with so much time to fill in, I sometimes imagined that I could see our ship from high above, as if I were an angel. I saw clearly how tiny we were in the immense space of the ocean. How was it possible for us to survive? I knew that the wood of the vessel kept the water out and that the engine drove us forward and that the skill of the captain kept us on course, but there was surely more keeping us alive than these things. One thing was our longing for freedom, so powerful. But another thing was the love of God. It was a force I could feel just as I felt the heat of the sun on my head and my back.

More than two weeks from the time we left the jetty, we encountered our first storm. It came up out of the hazy distance as a patch of grey, then it became black. The first winds struck with incredible force, knocking people off their feet so that they had to grasp whatever part of the fixtures on deck would hold them. But these winds were gentle compared to what followed them. The sea rose in immense hills. The boat plunged down so low in the troughs of the waves that I feared we would be smashed into pieces of matchwood. People fled below deck, waiting for death. I stayed on deck, holding tight to the structure of the hut that housed the captain. Never in my life had I seen such fury from man or nature. It was like warfare.

A woman made her way onto the deck from below, struggling with all her might to keep her feet. She held tightly to her breast a tiny baby.

'In God's name, sister, go below!' I screamed at her, but she paid me no attention. She braced herself close to me, holding the same structure that I was relying on. She called out with all the force of her heart and soul, loud enough to rise above the shrieking of the winds and the crashing of the waves. And what she cried out was this:

'Allah the beloved, I have sinned in my life but my child has not! Spare my child, I beg you!'

She cried this out again and again, battling the waves and the winds. I watched in wonder, deeply moved by her fervour and courage. She was a skinny creature and did not look strong, but her love of her child had given her immense strength. She held her head high, struggling not only to hold her infant and herself on deck, but struggling also to keep her head covered. The wind tore at her black garments as if enraged by her courage and her pleas. I expected at any moment to see her lifted into the air and flung on the stormy surface of the ocean.

At last the wind began to lose its force. It happened little by little. One moment I was using every ounce of my strength to hold myself on the deck, then five minutes or so later I was able to stand upright. The Iraqi woman settled onto her knees, sobbing tears of gratitude and stroking the head of her baby.

Although the storm had passed, the sea remained rough. The boat heaved on the swell and descended into the troughs. I could hear no engine sound and sought out the captain for an explanation. His customary response to every crisis was to shrug. 'Broken,' he said in Dari. The crew dropped anchor, which was puzzling to me, but I was told that we were close to a reef and that the anchor would reach the bottom. I had no idea what a reef was, and it seemed unlikely to me that there was any bottom to the ocean.

People made their way onto the deck, looking amazed still to be alive. One after another, they raised their hands to Heaven and cried, 'By the grace of God, whom we bless!' No doubt they also gave the captain great credit for saving them from the storm, but I was certain myself that the captain was as surprised by his craft's survival as I was.

For the remainder of that day, the boat remained almost stationary in the swell. Many of the passengers, suffering from seasickness after the storm and still exhausted after so many hours of dread, went below deck to sleep and prepare for whatever the next ordeal might be. I preferred to stay on deck. Such a strange man as our captain might well decide to jump overboard or grow wings and fly away to the netherworld where he was spawned, and I did not want to wake up and find myself abandoned.

In the middle of the night, I felt the boat moving, even though the engine was silent. I grabbed one of the crewmen who could speak a little Dari and demanded to know what was happening.

'The anchor is gone,' he said.

'Gone where?'

'Who knows? The chain broke.'

I ran to the captain and asked him what he intended to do now that the anchor had gone. Once again, he shrugged. What a strange man! So far as I could see, he had no interest in anything, not even in living.

The boat finally came to a dead stop in the light of morning within sight of clumps of some strange matter peering above the top of the ocean. This strange matter was, so I was told, a reef made of coral.

'Coral? What is coral?' I asked the crewman. He said, 'It grows in the sea.' I was baffled. It seemed to me that the ocean was an entirely different world, full of astonishing creatures and strange powers. I learned a little later that this growth of the ocean had a name, and was called 'Ashmore'.

For days we sat on the ocean by the coral reefs of Ashmore. The captain and the four crewmen had no plans for repairing the boat and continuing the journey. So far as I could see, they were content to die. Passengers looked at each other in alarm, with the alarm growing as the days passed. Had we given ourselves into the care of madmen? For myself, I could not believe that we were all going to die out here in the ocean—not even when our food and fresh water were almost gone. Why would God end my story in such a way? He was not wasteful, so why would He have allowed me to survive the Russians, the communists, the mujahedin, the Taliban and a mighty storm on this huge ocean only to fade away in silence in the coral land of Ashmore? I felt so strongly His interest in me and in all of us on this vessel, and why would He have remained so interested in us if He intended to turn His gaze to another part of the world at this late hour? No, whatever final fate God had in mind for me, I felt certain that it was not this fate.

I was right to believe that we had God's attention, for out of the blue sky on the morning of our fifth day at Ashmore came an aeroplane. We first heard the sound of its engines, then saw the aeroplane itself, flying in low from the south-west. It passed overhead, bringing every person aboard our boat onto the deck. We tore our shirts off and waved them and shouted at the tops of our voices, 'We are here! Save us, in the name of your God whom we honour as we honour Allah Himself!' The plane passed overhead again, close enough for us to see strange letters and signs on its underside. Then it headed away again to the south-east, and many of us on the boat, and I was amongst them, fell to our knees and hammered the planks of the deck in despair. When I had recovered, I looked for the captain to ask him if the aeroplane would return. I found him sitting in his hut, cutting calluses from his feet with a fishing knife.

'Will the aeroplane return?' I demanded.

He shrugged. 'Who knows?' he said, and continued working on his ugly feet.

I returned to the place on the deck that I had made my home for the whole of the voyage—a small space near the bow. I closed my eyes and put my head on my knees. I spoke not to God, but to my mother and brothers and sister, and especially to Hakima and to the baby Maria. I spoke about the ocean and the storm and about the aeroplane that had flown above us. I had a great need to talk, to free my mind of the anxiety of waiting. When I addressed Hakima, I said, 'Ah, if you could see me! I am floating on the ocean near to a land called Ashmore. It grew by itself in the ocean!' Every few minutes, I looked up from my conversations to study the horizon. I saw nothing until, without warning, the voice of our silent captain, never heard above a mutter, was raised in a great shout. I did not realise it was the captain at first, but then I saw him on the roof of his hut, waving the cloth he wore around his head. What he was shouting I didn't understand, nor did I see what had made him shout in this way. But then I saw, coming out of the heat haze a ship; a ship much, much bigger than ours, much more beautiful. Within seconds everybody was shouting and so many had run to the side of the boat that our vessel dipped dangerously. Others had picked up the word that the captain was shouting, and at last I understood. They were shouting, 'Australia! Australia!' I waved as madly as anyone, and I, too, shouted, 'Australia!' more loudly than I had shouted anything in my life.

23

Impossible Things

IT IS FOUR O'CLOCK in the morning. I have been awake for two hours. I sit on the sofa in the living room of the flat drinking tea. Colin will arrive before long. He is a very reliable friend, and one of many, many friends I have made in the rug business, but as special to me as Robin. His advice to me on business, on life, always goes straight to my heart. And he said he would come at a certain time, and he surely will.

I can hear the sound of cars and trucks on Dandenong Road half a kilometre away. Not so many cars and trucks at this early time of the morning, but a few. I turn on the television with the remote control but even before the picture appears on the screen, I turn it off again. I am nervous even though I have nothing to be nervous about.

I walk about the flat, taking my tea with me. I stand at the door of the big bedroom and look in at the new furniture. I open the door of the other bedroom, the smaller one, and smile. The single bed is made up neatly.

I have brought a few things home from the shop for the flat, but not many. The flat looks like many other flats in this block, I am sure. I have not tried to make it into an Afghani household. It is comfortable and clean. That is what is important. When I first looked at it with the estate agent a few months ago all that I wanted was a clean place, a comfortable place, a place not so far from my shop in High Street. This suburb is Windsor, only a short distance from High Street.

I sit down on the sofa again and look at my watch. Ten minutes past four. Surely Colin will arrive soon.

I try to relax. I sit back on the sofa, holding my teacup in both hands. I sip from the cup, then close my eyes. What do I wish to think about? Business, maybe? The shop is doing well. It is my shop now, completely mine. I have bought out my partner. The stock is splendid. In the display window I have a big tribal rug with an elephant foot design. And how many rugs stacked neatly along the walls in piles more than a metre high? Perhaps 500. Some are of great quality, others I keep for people who don't have a lot of money to spend. I have 20 rugs and kilims displayed on the walls. When people wander into my shop, they stand and gaze around and smile. I don't want to sound too proud, but the shop is truly beautiful. Most customers do not know very much about rugs, and it is my pleasure to explain a few things to them. Not too much. I have kept my promise that I made in Woomera about letting the customers simply look at the rugs and enjoy the beauty of them. I am not pushy, not shalla. Sometimes I have to use all of my willpower to keep quiet, though. If a customer says something a little bit ignorant,

I want to correct him. If he says, 'I've seen a better rug than this, and cheaper, just down the road,' I want to say, 'Excuse me, sir, but this is a rug made from the finest fleece in Afghanistan. The rug you saw down the road—and I know the one you mean—is made from dog hair.' But I say no such thing. I smile and make a few points about the texture and the quality of the dyes and the tautness of the weave and the magnificence of the design, and let it go at that. Most people enjoy learning about the rugs they are looking at, but some don't. Fine, let them buy dog-hair rugs for their home.

But no, I don't want to think about business. Then what do I wish to think about while I am waiting for Colin? Maybe about something that is impossible; about a small secret room the size of a cupboard in my friend's house, and my cousin Gassem and I bunched into that small space with the sweat of fear running down our faces, and outside men in white robes and white turbans armed with AK47s whose great project is to find Hazara like Gassem and me and shoot them. Is it possible that I was able to leave that secret room and put on the white robes and white turban of the men who wanted to shoot me, and so escape? Is it possible that I passed 20 or more checkpoints without being dragged from the vehicle in which I was escaping and shot on the roadside? Is it possible that I journeyed for thousands of kilometres to the strange country of Indonesia, and then travelled in a boat that was already sinking before 96 fearful people climbed aboard and somehow reached the land of Ashmore that had grown out of the sea? Is it possible that I was put into the prison of Woomera and sat trembling in the room of questions and then one glorious day was told by the Canberra Australians that I could stay? Did I find work for my hands and work for my brain? Did I learn to speak the language of Australia? Did I find a shop, and fill the shop with rugs of great beauty and survive the torture of the GST? Am I now only two and a half hours away from the most wonderful thing in the world? Is any of this possible? No, it is all impossible, it is all daydreams. But it is true.

A car horn honks, just outside my flat. I sit up quickly, spilling the last of my tea.

* * *

Colin drives me up St Kilda Road and past Flinders Street Station and Federation Square and down Flinders Street to Elizabeth Street and through the city to Flemington Road and down Flemington Road to the Tullamarine Freeway. As we speed along the freeway, the first light of morning comes into the sky.

Colin says, 'Great day, mate,' and I say, 'Yes, mate, a great day.' Colin turns on the radio. The voice of a lady says, 'All the freeways are running like a charm, not a problem in sight, but drivers are reminded that the left lane inbound on the Westgate is closed for maintenance, surprise surprise.' Another voice, that of a man, says, 'Thanks for that, Hilary. And now I've got Jim on the line...'

I watch the light growing brighter in the sky. Colin looks across at me. He sees the tears in my eyes.

'Take it easy, mate,' he says. Then he says again, 'Great day, eh?'

Colin stops at the ticket machine and presses the red button. He takes the ticket and puts it in his coat pocket. He drives up to the first level of the car park, then to the second and finds a parking place near the lifts. We walk down the stairs instead of waiting for the lift and cross one road and then another and enter the airport building. It is as bright inside as the middle of the day. People are waiting in lines with their suitcases and a voice is announcing something about Singapore Airlines. Colin stops below a board that tells us when aeroplanes arrive and leave. I hold up a piece of paper that I have had in my hand since Colin picked me up from my flat in Windsor. We both look at the letters and numbers on the paper and search for the same letters and numbers on the board above us. Colin says, 'It's landed, mate. Give them 45 minutes, Customs, Immigration. Cup of tea?'

We sit in a café and sip our tea from red cups. I want to light a cigarette but Colin says no. 'Have a SWAT team on us, mate. Worse crime than terrorism. Throw you on a plane and send you back to the Taliban.'

'How long now?' I ask.

'Ooh, about 20 minutes.'

'Come,' I say, and I grab his arm and make him take me through all the people with their suitcases to the waiting place. We stand at the front of a big crowd beside a young woman and a man holding up a sign that says, 'Chooka!' Other people are holding up signs, many other people. I am worried that I should be holding up a sign myself.

Now people are coming out of the doors before us, pushing trolleys loaded up high with suitcases and bundles. As they come out, they stop and look at the crowd and when they see those waiting for them, their faces break into smiles.

I am counting the people who have come out of the doors. At 70, I begin to grow more anxious.

Colin says, 'She'll be right.'

I wish I had made a sign. The man and the woman beside me hold their sign up high above their heads each time the doors open and more people with trolleys of suitcases come out. Then the person they are waiting for comes through the doors and the girl calls out, 'Chooka! Chooka!' and begins to cry.

How many people can an aeroplane carry? I have counted up to 190. Surely there has been a disaster. Colin puts his arm around my shoulders.

'Easy, mate, easy,' he says.

When Hakima and Maria come through the doors, I cry out in Dari, 'Blessings! Blessings!' then I close my eyes just for two seconds and give thanks to God. My wife and daughter haven't seen me yet. I lean forward over the rail and wave my arms. Hakima is pushing a trolley loaded high, and on top of the bundles sits Maria. She is smiling with all of her white teeth, but when she sees me, she looks alarmed and scrambles back to Hakima and throws her arms around her. Perhaps I look like a madman to her. Hakima steers her trolley to the rail and talks softly to me. I touch Maria's hair and say her name, and she lifts her face and looks at me. I walk along on my side of the rail, excusing myself to the other people still waiting. Maria watches me from her side of the rail. By the time Hakima reaches the end of the rail, Maria is smiling and allows me to lift her in my arms.

Colin says, 'You going to introduce me, you rude bastard?'

'Sorry,' I say. 'Sorry. Hakima, my wife, and my daughter Maria.' And I add, in Dari, 'This is my friend, Colin.'

'Welcome to Australia,' says Colin.

Colin pushes the trolley while I walk with Hakima beside me

and Maria in my arms. I cannot describe the feeling in my heart. Impossible things have become possible. Hakima and Maria have travelled here from the north of Pakistan where Afghanis in their thousands do not even permit themselves to dream of peace and security.

Young men with hearts full of rage walk the refugee camps, hungry to find a cause to kill for and to die for. One of the most important lessons in life for the children is to recognise signs that warn of land mines. A baby born in one of these camps today has hardly any chance of one day sitting in a classroom listening to a teacher talking about a visit to the zoo. By good fortune that I deserve no more than any other Afghani in those refugee camps, I can think of Maria studying her school lessons and growing wiser with each year. She may want to go to the university in Carlton. She may become a doctor, or maybe even a teacher herself. I pray that the worst she will see of the world she has already seen, and what she has seen will fade from her mind.

When we leave the airport terminal through the sliding glass doors, morning has filled the sky. All sorts of people are going about their business, hurrying or dawdling. Yellow taxis in a long line are filling with customers who have just arrived from countries all over the world. I see Muslim women dressed in a very traditional way, and young Muslim women in jeans and T-shirts with no more than a stylish scarf to show their religion. A group of young men and girls with backpacks are laughing together at the bus stop. Men with walkie-talkies and orange vests are organising the people in the taxi queue. No policemen to be seen, no soldiers with guns.

'Wait,' I say to Colin, and he turns and looks at me. He can see that nothing is wrong; that it is just my happiness.

'Take your time,' he says.

I stand just where I am outside the doors of the terminal with Maria in my arms, and with Hakima taking pleasure in the pleasure I am taking in holding our daughter.

I use this minute—before we go to the car park and drive back to the flat in Windsor—to honour Gorg Ali and Rossal Ali and my uncle and cousin who were set on fire. Not all of us were able to survive the wars of Afghanistan. Let my good fortune do justice to them. Impossible things have happened. Dreams that were dreamt in Afghanistan have put down roots in the soil of another nation, and today I see buds forming on twigs and branches.

'Let's go,' I say to Colin. 'What are we waiting for?'

Postscript

THE FLAG OF AFGHANISTAN is black, red and green, with a picture of a mosque at the centre. The mosque is surrounded by sheaves of wheat in a circle, and by sacred writing in both Arabic and Dari. Whenever I see this flag, I know that it represents my homeland. And I know that my homeland is a big country, huge, and that it has borders with no fewer than six other nations, and that it has its capital city at Kabul. Afghanistan has its own national anthem, too, played at the Olympic Games. But a flag and borders and a capital city and a national anthem do not really make a homeland. Far more important to me than the colours and design of the Afghan flag are the patterns in rugs that came into being over thousands of years; patterns that change from region to region. More important than the national anthem of Afghanistan are the songs sung by Afghanis for centuries that tell of love and harvests and war and death and changing seasons and hope. My homeland is the taste in my mouth of certain dishes that have been prepared in Mazar-e-Sharif for ages, and the rich smell of the herbs my mother uses in cooking. My homeland is also the great size of the full moon just after sunset, the colour of wildflowers, the expressions on the faces of people who share my history, the way these people smile or laugh, and the language that they speak—a language that my tongue and lips began to learn just as my small legs were learning to take their first steps.

Australia can never be my homeland because I started here too late. I had already fallen in love with my part of Afghanistan, and I will be faithful for life. But if Australia is not my homeland, it is certainly my home. This is a land that I have learnt to love in a way that is different from my love for Afghanistan. This is a land I love for its kindness to me, for the chance it gave me to rebuild my dreams. This is the land where the most generous people I will ever know smiled at me and said, 'How can we help you, Najaf?' Australia is a land that I love in the way that a man loves the friend who saved his life.

I have been to Pakistan three times since the days of Woomera. I go back to look at rugs, buy rugs, see with my own eyes the quality of what I am purchasing. My family journeys from Mazar-e-Sharif to see me in Pakistan, and I have taken each member of my family in my arms. My friends in Mazar-e-Sharif say to me, 'You are a fortunate man, Najaf.' Whenever Muslims speak of good fortune, we always remember to thank God, the One who fashions fortune with His mind and His hands. I have stood shaking my head many times about this business of good fortune. Too many Afghanis have not been blessed in the way I have been blessed. Why was I chosen to prosper? Why did my troubles catch the eye of God? It is a puzzle that can never be answered.

Not in Mazar-e-Sharif, but elsewhere, the Taliban has returned. My friends in Afghanistan talk about this return without any surprise. The Taliban fighters are very stubborn. When I watch the news on the ABC and SBS and I hear that the people who killed so many Hazara and who wanted to kill me are gaining strength in the south, I shake my head and wonder how long it will be before they reach the north. I hear the Americans talking about the war on terrorism, and about how it will take a long time to win that war. But the Americans and the Australians and other Western countries with soldiers in Afghanistan do not really understand what 'a long time' means. They think it means ten years, maybe. They think ten years is a very long time to be fighting. But the Taliban fighters think that ten years is nothing. Even a hundred years is not a long time. The American soldiers have lives to return to in America, just as the Australian soldiers have lives in Australia. But the Taliban fighters have only their mission, which is victory. I have reason to worry that my country will be at war for a long time to come. This is not new. Very few Afghanis can remember a time when there was no fighting. And so it will always be important to me that I am an Australian; that I have a friend in the world.

I am an Australian on paper, not just in my head. I have a certificate to prove it. I dressed in a suit with a long, Afghan shirt beneath my jacket and went to Malvern Town Hall to receive my citizenship certificate. Hakima and Maria came with me, and like me they smiled for the whole time and could not stop smiling for hours afterwards. A lady from *The Age* newspaper by the name of Sushi Das interviewed me. She asked me about my life in Afghanistan, and she asked me why I had taken the risk of coming to Australia. I was too happy to speak at great length of terrible things, but I told her that I came for Maria. I told her that it should not be necessary for children to worry about bullets in the street and rockets from the air. Sushi had brought a photographer with her by the name of Joseph. He took many pictures of me and in all of the pictures, I was smiling over my whole face. The people who read my story in the paper must have thought all the things I said about bombs and violence were fantasies. 'Could a man who has run for his life leaping the bodies of the dead smile in this way? Surely not!'

I was one of many new citizens at the ceremony, some from countries in Asia, some from South America, some, like me, from the Middle East. Many had brought friends along to watch. I was not asked to tell the world that Australia is the best country on earth, I was not asked to make myself ready to fight people in the streets with an automatic rifle, I was not asked to say that I loved the Prime Minister. I was asked only to obey the laws of Australia, and I gladly agreed to that. After the ceremony, a party was held for me by my friend Robin at her house, not so far from Malvern Town Hall. The party was crowded with people I had not known anything about five years earlier, and who had not known of my existence. These people, all of them, were now my friends, and many had made it their job to help me build a new life. Speeches were made. Many kind things were said about me. When it was my turn to speak, I gave my thanks to all of my friends. Later in the evening, I looked around at all of the people. I thought once again, 'Why have I had this good fortune? Why?' I thought of all the people in Afghanistan who would never know such happiness and enjoy such safety. If it was possible, I would bring all of the people who need safety to Australia, but that is daydreaming. Even as

I smiled and laughed with my friends at Robin's house, people in Afghanistan who deserved good fortune for the hard work they had accepted all their lives were dying. And so a cloud of sadness made its home over my head for a time, and my smiles were polite smiles, they did not come from my heart. But when I saw my daughter shining like the sun, the cloud sped away. I cannot forget the Afghanis who have not met with good fortune, and I never will. But I will never forget the sunshine of Maria's smile on the day of the party, either.

نقشے علی مزاری   Ahmad

* * *

*One way in which I try to solve the problem of my good
fortune is to share it in every way I can with those in
Mazar-e-Sharif who need some comfort in their lives.
I have joined with friends to start a fund that will
build schools and buy ambulances for the people of
Mazar-e-Sharif. I am not the United Nations, but surely
I can help in a small way. Helping in small ways is good.
I really appreciate my Australian friends who have helped
me set up the Mazar Development Fund which you can
find at www.mazardevelopmentfund.org.au*

Acknowledgements

The most enjoyable part of telling this story has arrived. I now have the chance to say how grateful I am to all the people who helped me build a new life in Australia. Each of the people I am about to mention has a home in my heart forever. Readers of this story will see only a list of names, but for me, each name shines like a star.

David Baillieu; Peter Bedwell; Peter Bennett; Robin and Norman Bourke; Julian Burnside; Tanya and Tracey Caulfield; Bryan Dawe; Kate Durham; Jeanie Gibb; Sally Godinho; Michael Gordon; Christian and Elisabeth Groves; Norm Groves; Bruce and Rea Hearn-Mackinnon; Wahid and Nadda El-Khoury; Harry Kontos; Yvonne Lawrence; Stephen Martin; Ahmad Raza; Christopher Remmer; Sylvie Shaw; Simon Stewart; Joan Sullivan; Dunstan Towning; Pamela Vincent; Colin Young; Phillip Young; all the wonderful people who helped me at the Asylum Seeker Resource Centre in Melbourne and Amnesty International Australia.

I never dreamt that I would publish my story, and for that opportunity, there are many people to thank. Firstly, there is my 'first Australian mother', Robin, who helped me learn English and who started writing down the events of my life. Then my dear friend Sylvie brought her friends who happened to be publishers – Iris Breuer and Cathi Lewis – who started talking to Robin. After many get-togethers over Afghani food and cardamom tea, Insight Publications commissioned Robert Hillman to write my story. Close friendships have flourished and I thank Iris and Cathi, Robert, the editors, the designer, the lovely people at Insight Publications, and everyone else for their time and talents. This is all very amazing for someone who could only go to school for three and a half years. My family overseas does not believe it is possible for me to have a book published, so you can imagine how much I want to send them copies to prove it's all true. So thank you everyone: this is my biggest dream.

Insight Publications and Najaf Mazari would like to express our very special gratitude to Robert Hillman. His sensitive and beautiful rendering of Najaf's story, unfolding as it did over many cups of tea and amongst a multitude of traditional Afghan rugs, truly gives voice to a remarkable man, and reaches into our hearts and our consciences.

We also wish to thank Mr Daoud Yaqub from the Centre for Arab and Islamic Studies at the Australian National University. At the eleventh hour, Mr Yaqub very kindly agreed to check historical and political references in the manuscript.

Glossary & Notes

ABC

Australian Broadcasting Corporation – Australia's publicly-funded national television and radio network.

Abdul Ali Mazari

Politician and champion for the Hazara people, campaigning for their representation in government. He gave guarded support to the Northern Alliance in its struggle with the Taliban in the early 1990s. When the Taliban forces gained control of large regions of Afghanistan, Abdul Ali Mazari was able to resist them and even managed to defeat them in a crucial battle. In March 1995, he was murdered by the Taliban at a meeting called to discuss a possible cease-fire.

AK47

Abbreviation for Russian-made Kalashnikov (1947) automatic rifle.

Allah

Muslim (Arabic) term for God.

Arabic

Principal language of all Arabic countries, and also spoken as a second language in some non-Arabic countries. The Koran, the holy book of Islam, is written in Arabic.

Ashmore Reef

Coral reef north of Australia where Najaf's boat was stranded.

ATO

Australian Taxation Office.

Babrak Karmal (1929–1996)

President of Afghanistan from 1979 until 1986. He had a long history in left-wing politics before being installed in the leadership position by the USSR (Union of Soviet Socialist Republics). After his government was overthrown following the defeat of the Russian military campaign in Afghanistan, he fled to Moscow where he lived out the rest of his life.

Bagh-e-Zanana Park

Park in Mazar-e-Sharif, literally translated as 'Women's Park'. That is only its name, however – it is open to everyone.

Baluchi rugs

Rugs that have been woven for centuries by Baluchi tribal weavers in southwest Pakistan, northeast Iran and northwest Afghanistan, and are mostly geometric in design. The Baluchi tree-of-life prayer rug is the best known pattern; others include repeating floral motifs or abstracts of living creatures such as animals and birds.

BAS

Abbreviation for the Business Activity Statement that all businesses in Australia are required to submit regularly throughout the year to the Australian Taxation Office.

Baubau

Small Indonesian coastal town from which the small fishing boat carrying Najaf and 95 other refugees sailed for Australia.

Blue Mosque

One of several names for this famous mosque in Mazar-e-Sharif which is covered with strikingly beautiful blue ceramic tiles. Its proper name is Rawze-e-Sharif (see later entry).

Borya grass

Type of grass used in constructing the roof when building mudbrick houses in Afghanistan. The grass is laid over a timber frame on the rafters and the mud is laid on top. The grass is also laid on the earthen floors, then kilims are placed on top.

Burka

Also spelt 'burqa'. Traditional garment that covers the whole body and is worn by some Muslim women over day clothes when they are outside the house. After the Taliban took power in Afghanistan in 1996, strict laws were introduced requiring all women, when in public, to wear an older style of the burka, called the chadri, which also completely covers the head and face. Officially, it is not required under the present Afghan regime, but local warlords still enforce its use in southern Afghanistan.

Cadre

Term meaning basic unit or group (or member of it) of activists in a revolutionary party (in this case, the Taliban); it also often refers to a military-type unit.

Canberra

Capital city of Australia and therefore the place where all Australian government departments are located. In this story, when Najaf refers to the 'Canberra Australians', he means the people in the Department of Immigration and Youth Affairs (now called the Department of Immigration and Citizenship) who are responsible for assessing refugee applications for entry to Australia.

CCTV

Closed-circuit television.

Chechens

People from Chechnya which was part of the Soviet Union. Since 1990, thousands of Chechens have fled their country seeking asylum as refugees from the ongoing violent conflict between the Russian government and those Chechens seeking independence.

Daira

Tambourine-like traditional Afghan drum used to accompany folk songs and dance music.

Dari

Official language of Afghanistan derived from ancient Persian and similar to Farsi, the language of Iran.

Deobandi

Fundamentalist branch of Islam. It emerged in the 1860s as a radical political and religious independence movement of Indian Muslims rebelling against the British occupation of their country. In recent decades, many members of the Taliban have come from the numerous Deobandi religious schools, or madrassas, that have proliferated in northern Pakistan along the border with Afghanistan. These schools are open to boys only, mainly drawing their students from the poorest communities and refugee camps in this region; they teach a strict form of Islam.

Farsi

Language spoken in Iran, which is very similar to Dari.

Fasoor

Popular card game played in Afghanistan and neighbouring countries.

Fis Kut

Card game played in Afghanistan and neighbouring countries.

Halal

Arabic word, often translated as 'clean', but actually means 'permissible' according to the laws of Islam. So it can apply to food – for instance, pork is never 'permissible' for eating, but other meat such as goat, lamb, beef or chicken are, as long as they are killed according to Islamic practices. Halal can also apply to clothing and behaviour, money, etc.

Hamal

First month of the Afghan calendar year which starts on 21 March in the Western calendar.

Haram

Arabic word which is usually translated as 'unclean' or 'forbidden'.

Hazara

Third largest ethnic group in Afghanistan, making up around 20% of the population. It is widely accepted that their ancestors came from Mongolia in the 13th and 14th centuries during the period of the Mongol Empire. The Hazaras are the most oppressed minority in Afghanistan, being Shi'a in a largely Sunni Muslim country and facing longstanding discrimination and persecution from other ethnic groups, particularly the ruling Pashtuns. The majority of Afghani boat people arriving in Australia during the Taliban regime were Hazara because they were particularly targeted by the (mainly Pashtun) Taliban.

Hazarajat

Mountainous region in central Afghanistan. It was settled by the

Hazaras in the 13th century and covers approximately 30% of the country. The main city is Baminyan, but it also includes Mazar-e-Sharif.

Islam

Religion of the Muslims who believe their faith was revealed through Mohammed, the prophet of Allah (God). It was founded on the Arabian Peninsula in the 7th century. There are close to two billion Muslims worldwide, mainly in North Africa, the Middle East and parts of Asia. The two main branches are Sunni and Shi'a.

Kabul

Capital city of Afghanistan which has existed for more than 3,000 years. It has been destroyed and built a number of times throughout its history.

Kalashnikov

Russian-made automatic rifle.

Kandahar

Second largest city of Afghanistan. Alexander the Great founded this city in the 4th century BC and named it Alexandria.

Khar plant

Refers to the Khar Buzh Khora, a prickly plant which goats eat that has wound-healing properties; also prevents skin from cracking in the cold.

Kilim

Woven carpet without a pile, mainly made by tribal peoples in a number of countries including Afghanistan, India, Turkey, Kurdistan and Iran.

Koran

Also Qur'an. The holy book of Islam which Muslims believe is the revelation of Allah to the prophet Mohammed, written in Arabic during his lifetime.

Kurd

Member of an ethnic minority group which has been fighting for independence for many years. Kurds live in a region straddling the borders of four countries: Turkey, Iraq, Iran and Syria.

Main Camp

Largest camp in the Woomera Detention Centre. Najaf goes there after being in Mike.

Mazar-e-Sharif

Najaf Mazari's home city in northern Afghanistan – famous for its blue mosque and its shrine, the reputed burial place of Ali, cousin and son-in-law of the prophet Mohammed.

Mike

A camp in the Woomera Detention Centre.

Mujahedin

Also spelt 'mujahideen'. Loosely-aligned Afghan guerilla groups, which came to prominence when they fought against the pro-Soviet Afghan government during the late 1970s. In 1979, when Soviet troops entered Afghanistan at the request of the Afghan government, the mujahedin forces fought both the Russian and Afghan government troops with marked success. After the Soviet Union pulled out of the conflict in the late 1980s, the mujahedin fought each other in the subsequent Afghan Civil War.

The 'Mule'

Nickname for the delivery truck in the Woomera Detention Centre.

Mullah

Muslim man who is a religious teacher or leader, trained in the doctrine and law of Islam; the head of a mosque.

Muslim

Follower of the Islamic religion.

Northern Alliance

Alliance also called the 'United Islamic Front for the Salvation of Afghanistan' (Western media used the term 'Northern Alliance'). This was formed from the warring factions of northern Afghanistan to prevent the Taliban taking over the country when they gained control of around 90% of Afghanistan.

November

Camp in the Woomera Detention Centre; Najaf's first camp.

Pashtun

Largest ethnic group in Afghanistan – about 42% of the population. They have been the most powerful group in that country for over 250 years. Around 15% of the population of Pakistan is also Pashtun.

Rawze-e-Sharif

Traditional name for the blue mosque which is set on over 100 acres of gardens and grounds in Mazar-e-Sharif.

Rubab

A short-necked string instrument that has a deep resonant sound; similar to a lute made of wood with a goatskin covering. The rubab (also 'rabab'), sometimes considered the national instrument of Afghanistan, is often called the 'lion' of instruments; it has a double-chambered body carved from mulberry wood, three main strings and a plectrum made from ivory, bone or wood.

Salaam

Greeting, 'Peace be upon you' in Arabic; used throughout the Middle East and in Muslim countries. Linguistically it is related to the Hebrew greeting, 'Shalom', which has the same meaning.

Serai

Very basic inn in the countryside. Guests all sleep together in the same room on mattresses on the floor or on a large raised platform. Shepherds or farmers moving their stock from one place to another are able to stay in these places overnight as there is a yard attached to hold any animals that guests might have.

Shalla

Colloquial term used in Mazar-e-Sharif (and possibly other areas of Afghanistan) meaning 'pushy'.

Shar Shar

Village in the Charkent region where Najaf Mazari spent his early childhood.

Shi'a

One of the two major branches of Islam – Sunni and Shi'a – which

260

formed after a split in the early years of the faith, and based on fundamental differences in beliefs. At times, these differences have led to major conflicts between the followers of the two major branches of Islam. Shi'ites make up only about 20% of Muslims worldwide.

Shrine of Ali

Shrine of Ali, the cousin and son-in-law of the prophet Mohammed, is the most famous shrine in Mazar-e-Sharif.

Sierra

Camp in the Woomera Detention Centre where people were sent if they were considered to have misbehaved or caused trouble.

Sunni

Numerically the dominant Muslim denomination. The Hazara are Shi'a but the majority of the population of Afghanistan is Sunni.

Tajikistan

Country bordering Afghanistan.

Talib

Arabic word meaning 'student' (the Taliban see themselves as students of the Koran).

Taliban

In power in Afghanistan from 1996-2001; achieved its success by opposing the anarchy and chaos into which Afghanistan had descended after the overthrow of the Soviet-backed government and the ensuing civil war that left thousands of Afghanis dead. The regime, based on strict fundamentalist beliefs, became notorious for its inhumane subjugation of women, the torture and massacre of thousands of its citizens, particularly of the Hazara, and its support of radical Islamic movements in other countries. The Taliban was ousted from power by the US-led invasion of Afghanistan in 2001, but has since re-established itself in the south of the country and continues guerrilla warfare against the present government of Afghanistan.

Tambor

Ancient stringed instrument with a long slender neck. It is known throughout central Asia and dates back to 1500 BC. Today it is mostly played in Afghanistan and Kurdistan to accompany popular music, but it was a holy instrument used by Sufi mystics and poets in Afghanistan.

Taskera

Twenty-page identity document, more common in Afghanistan than passports. It has now been replaced with a Taskera Certificate, also called a National Identification Card, which can be obtained from Afghanistan and used by Afghanis who need to confirm that they are legal citizens of Afghanistan.

Temporary Protection Visa – TPV

Three-year temporary visa issued by the Australian government to unauthorised arrivals. The granting of the TPV carries with it certain rights and support to help people settle in their new country. Controversy surrounded the decision not to grant TPVs to 'illegal asylum seekers', that is, to those who have fled their countries with the help of people smugglers and who have bypassed countries that might have offered protection. This has meant that people with refugee status according to UN and Human Rights Laws may not be given refugee status in Australia. This withholding of TPVs from newly-arrived asylum seekers has drawn criticism from international Human Rights groups.

Toishak

Mattress used in Afghanistan.

Tula

Traditional Afghan musical instrument similar to a large recorder. It has six finger holes and is played by blowing into, or across, the mouthpiece.

United Front

'United Islamic Front for the Salvation of Afghanistan', also referred to as the Northern Alliance by Western media. It was an umbrella organisation that united various Afghan factions fighting against each other so that they could be more effective in resisting the Taliban.

Wahhabism

'Wahhabism' takes its name from the Saudi Arabian Muslim scholar, Muhammad bin Abd al-Wahhab (1703–1791) who campaigned for a return to the fundamentals of Islam – hence 'fundamentalism' – as set out in the seventh-century teachings of the prophet Mohammed. 'Wahhabism' has developed into a movement that aims 'to purify' the Islamic religion of anything seen as a sign of moral decline.

Woomera Detention Centre

Woomera Immigration Reception and Processing Centre, located in a remote desert area 486 km north of Adelaide. It was one of several such centres set up to accommodate people who entered the country without a visa, often as 'boat people'. The detainees remained in detention centres until their applications for visas had been processed. By April 2000, Woomera housed 1,500 people, including women and children mainly from Afghanistan, Iraq and Iran. It had four main 'camps' or compounds. Its tall steel fencing topped with razor wire, for many people outside as well as within, represented a harsh and inhumane treatment of already traumatised people. Because of slow processing of information and a poor staff-to-detainee ratio, riots sometimes broke out and escapes of detainees from the centre became more common. Protestors from the general public also rallied there against the conditions endured by detainees at Woomera, and against what was seen as the injustice of Australia's immigration policy at that time. Woomera was officially closed on Thursday 17 April 2003.